A Bible for Today

A Bible for Today

An Abridged Version for Seekers and Survivors

ROBERT P. VANDE KAPPELLE

WIPF & STOCK · Eugene, Oregon

A BIBLE FOR TODAY
An Abridged Version for Seekers and Survivors

Copyright © 2022 Robert P. Vande Kappelle. All rights reserved. Except for brief quotations in critical publications or reviews, no part of this book may be reproduced in any manner without prior written permission from the publisher. Write: Permissions, Wipf and Stock Publishers, 199 W. 8th Ave., Suite 3, Eugene, OR 97401.

Wipf & Stock
An Imprint of Wipf and Stock Publishers
199 W. 8th Ave., Suite 3
Eugene, OR 97401

www.wipfandstock.com

PAPERBACK ISBN: 978-1-6667-5644-9
HARDCOVER ISBN: 978-1-6667-5645-6
EBOOK ISBN: 978-1-6667-5646-3

AUGUST 30, 2022 11:11 AM

Unless otherwise noted, Bible quotations are from the New Revised Standard Version of the Bible, copyright © 1989 by the Division of Christian Education of the National Council of the Churches of Christ in the United States of America. Used by permission.

To Ben and Emily

May your love of reading
include a passion for Scripture.
—Proverbs 3:5–6

Contents

Preface | ix

CHAPTER 1
 The Bible: Its Nature and Composition | 1

CHAPTER 2
 Scripture as Canonical Process | 19

CHAPTER 3
 Biblical Inspiration and Interpretation | 35

CHAPTER 4
 Biblical Versions and Translations | 54

CHAPTER 5
 Old Testament Literature, Part I: Overview and Passages | 71

CHAPTER 6
 Old Testament Literature, Part II: Overview and Passages | 86

CHAPTER 7
 New Testament Literature, Part I: Overview and Passages | 98

CHAPTER 8
 New Testament Literature, Part II: Overview and Passages | 114

APPENDIX
 Reading the (Abridged) Bible in Less than a Year:
 Daily Readings | 127

Bibliography | 133

Index | 135

Preface

How many times have we heard people say they have read the entire Bible, in some cases many times? As a child I participated with my parents in a ritual of daily Bible reading, occasionally at mealtimes and most often in the evening before going to bed. Raised in a missionary household, I had no television to watch, and so on nights when no church or evangelistic meetings were scheduled, we held our own devotional rituals at home. In addition to family devotions, I was encouraged to read the Bible on my own daily, and this habit led to an intimacy with scripture that shaped my identity. As I learned at home and as was confirmed at church, the Bible was God's authoritative Word, a guidebook for life, an aid to decision-making, a stimulus to evangelism, and a pathway to intimacy with God and fellow believers. Guided by the example of my mother, who read the entire Bible some seventy times, including English and Spanish versions, I too read through the Bible multiple times.

During childhood, adolescence, and early adulthood, the Bible was my constant companion. While initially I read it for guidance and encouragement, eventually I did it to gain biblical knowledge and expertise, for the Bible seemed inexhaustible in breadth and depth. As I discovered, there was always more to learn, not only in content but also in context and interpretation. My knowledge of scripture, fueled by my inquisitive and competitive nature, meant that I was rarely stumped on biblical trivia exams, and when it came to "sword drills" (a competition to see who could find biblical passages or references the fastest), whether in Sunday School, youth group, or church camp, I was practically invincible.

My fascination with the Bible continued during my undergraduate and graduate studies, and after completing bachelor and master's degrees, I enrolled in divinity studies at Princeton Theological Seminary, focusing on biblical studies, a program of study that culminated in doctoral studies with a dissertation on the intertestamental period and a focus on the relation between the Old and New Testaments.

READING SCRIPTURE

My love affair with scripture began at the age of four, lasted through a forty-year-teaching career in the field of religious and biblical studies, and has not wavered since. But why should we read the Bible, and why have some people devoted a lifetime to its study?

Christianity, the predominant, most accessible, and most diffuse of the world's religions, has arguably inspired the world's greatest art, music, and architecture. It has also inspired its most memorable speeches, sermons, and lectures; its most elevated theology and philosophy; and its most elegant rhetoric and prose. At the heart of this movement that has captured the imagination of people around the globe is its scripture, known as the Holy Bible, a library of books divided into testaments, one Jewish and the other Christian.

The Bible, the all-time best-selling book, is the most read, best known, most published, and most widely disseminated book in the world. Its value is inestimable, for it has single-handedly changed the course of world history, guiding empires, influencing legal systems, and impacting the lives of untold millions around the globe. Columbus took a copy to the New World, Charles Lindbergh stowed a copy in the cramped quarters of the Spirit of St. Louis on his epic trans-Atlantic flight, and astronaut James Irwin, who carried a copy on his moon walk, became the first person to quote from the Bible while on the moon: "I will lift up my eyes unto the hills, from whence cometh my help" (Ps 121:1, KJV).

For two thousand years this book, in part or in whole, has been viewed as sacred by generations of believers, its sacredness related not to the origin of the Bible but rather to its status within the Christian community. At the time of their composition, the books of the Bible were not considered to be part of scripture. Rather, the various parts of the Bible became sacred through canonization, a process that took several centuries. For Christians, the status of the Bible as sacred scripture means it is the primary collection of writings they know, definitive for faith and practice. The sacredness of scripture is validated by its ability to inspire believers in every age, thereby authenticating its enduring message.

Preface

Despite its influence, many readers find it ponderous and lengthy, and much of it seems incomprehensible, inaccessible, or irrelevant to modern society. Wishing to breach its defenses and to access its wisdom, many readers do an end run, picking and choosing best-known passages or portions that they find intriguing, Others read selectively, finding passages that support their beliefs or clarify doctrinal confusion. Some diehards, however, reading it as they might a novel, start at the beginning, attempting to read it from beginning to end. But they hit a wall around Exodus and Numbers, and certainly in Leviticus. Other more persistent readers might continue until 1 Chronicles, when nine chapters of genealogies bring their reading to a halt. By then, if they haven't lost interest altogether, they join the larger group of those content to focus on short passages or biblical books of their own choosing.

Worse than this is when seekers are told to begin with books such as the gospel of John or the book of Revelation that, when read literally, non-contextually, and apart from modern scholarship, can lead to extreme, unrealistic, and unhealthy fundamentalistic practices and belief systems.

To counter immature, skewed, or harmful attitudes regarding scripture, *A Bible for Today* offers an approach to biblical reading and study that is both valid and practical. Reading the passages and following the guidelines offered in ensuing chapters makes the Bible more readable to seekers, for it eliminates much of the redundancy in scripture, cuts its length nearly by half, and culminates in a program of short daily readings designed to make the Bible accessible and to acquaint modern readers with essential biblical passages and teachings in less than a year's time.

Throughout most of church history, the Bible was read primarily by religious scholars and liturgical officiants and only rarely by the general public. With the invention of the printing press by Johannes Gutenberg in the fifteenth century, the Bible became more accessible, and in the centuries following the Protestant Reformation, more widely read. The twentieth century witnessed a near revolution in biblical accessibility, appearing in a remarkable variety of versions and editions. In each case, whether through translation, paraphrase, adaptation, abridgment, and modernization, these editions were designed to reduce the Bible's excessive length, complexity, and obscurity, bringing its message ever closer to the mind and heart of the general reader.

In 1982, the Reader's Digest Association utilized the expertise of Bruce Metzger, my seminary professor and personal mentor, to produce

Preface

The Reader's Digest Bible, a condensed version based on the Revised Standard Version of the Bible, the latest and most scholarly version then available. The goal of that condensation was to reduce the biblical text by some 40 percent, achieved by reducing the text of the Old Testament by approximately one half and that of the New Testament by about one quarter. For those interested in a condensed version, committed on retaining the message and much of the wording of each text, paragraph, and chapter of every book of the Bible, I recommend that version for its accessibility, readability, and comprehension.

In *A Bible for Today*, I take a different approach, offering a Bible equally accessible, readable, and inspiring while keeping the essential message and storyline intact. I do so by eliminating not only repetitive passage, but also blocks of material that modern readers find irrelevant, boring, inappropriate, and no longer applicable. In ancient times, the device of repetition—in word, thought, and story—was highly valued for its rhetorical effect, but today such practices bore and confuse to most readers. Likewise, passages describing ancient Hebraic cultic laws and priestly practices hold little interest and relevance for people wishing to grow spiritually on a Christian foundation.

Throughout history, those who have attempted to change scripture in any way, whether through additions, subtractions, or modifications of any kind, have encountered hostility, been attacked, and their reputations smeared. Often, such attempts have been cloaked with condemnations from Revelation 22:19. Unfortunately, those who have done so have failed to realize that when the book of Revelation was written, it was not part of the Bible, so its warnings cannot be made to apply to scripture as a whole. Furthermore, they fail to understand that the author of Revelation intended his words to function as an ancient copyright, solely to protect his artistry. Lacking spiritual and theological merit, such words cannot be said to come from God. Furthermore, to those who might think that my intention is to add or subtract words, books, or passages to or from the Bible, that is simply not the case, for I only wish to provide readers of scripture a simplified method for reading the Bible. Readers seeking additional breadth and depth are encouraged to persevere with their desire.

In contrast to most abridgments and condensations of scripture, *A Bible for Today* provides a logical sequence of readings that readers can follow in whatever version they select. By dividing the readings into individual units, I provide an instrument whereby readers can move through

Preface

the Bible in eleven months, at a pace adaptable to the busiest schedule. All I ask is that readers devote some fifteen to twenty minutes a day for eleven months, a task aggressive readers can complete in five and a half months if they wish to double the time commitment or split their reading into two fifteen-minute blocks a day. Those who follow my method will discover that the readings reduce the Old Testament by 44 percent and the New Testament by 32 percent, for a total reduction of 41 percent of the biblical text.

My approach should not be considered "Bible light," for there is no attempt here to diminish the biblical message or to abbreviate or condense the biblical text. Rather, my sole intent is to eliminate primarily cultic material, oracles of doom to ancient nations, passages of gratuitous sex and/or violence, and excessively biased, racist, or exclusivist material, together with repetitive passages.

In addition to its inspirational quality, the Bible is great literature, and it is its ongoing message—encouraging, visionary, and hopeful in nature—that I wish to retain and highlight. In producing this work, my intention is altogether different from the "Jefferson Bible," entitled *The Life and Morals of Jesus of Nazareth*, an abridgement resulting from Thomas Jefferson's theological bias against miracles such as the resurrection and the deity of Christ. My abridgment, practical and helpful in nature, avoids bias while nurturing forms of spirituality primarily modern, pluralistic, and non-violent in nature. As you can imagine, approaching the Bible with preconceived intentions, such as Jefferson's approach, leads to flawed results, for it results in a Jesus and a Bible made in one's image and likeness and bypasses scripture's didactic nature altogether.

Aside from deleting certain segments inappropriate for young readers and immature Christians, such as passages excessively violent, vindictive, or sexually graphic, my intention has been to remain objective and free from doctrinal bias. As a bonus, I provide introductory overviews for each book of the Bible, succinct enough to be readable, yet literarily, historically, thematically, and theologically reliable and informative.

This book offers modern readers an ideal opportunity to become intimately acquainted with the biblical message and storyline while providing momentum for even the most skeptical and hesitant reader. In less than a year, readers can read through the Bible and know they have acquired a basic grasp of its individual and overall message. Building on this foundation, it is hoped that this encounter sparks in-depth reading and additional study in the future.

Preface

A Bible for Today is useful for individual or group study. The first four chapters conclude with questions suitable for discussion or reflection. As you read this book, consider journaling as a way to learn and understand. As you reflect and write, be honest with your thoughts and hopes, without ignoring your fears. In addition to the questions provided, individuals and group leaders are encouraged to add or substitute their own questions. The point of the reading is not to finish the assigned chapter or task, but rather to maintain momentum, that is, to keep the discussion fresh and vital and therefore open and ongoing. Upon concluding each chapter or session, readers and participants will profit by asking the question, "What is the primary insight I/we gained from this chapter or session?"

Chapter 1

The Bible: Its Nature and Composition

Humans are meaning-seeking creatures. Without some pattern or significance in their lives, humans fall easily into depression or despair. Language plays a vital role in our quest for meaning, helping us to communicate with others, certainly, but also enabling us to clarify our inner world. In this respect, language gives voice to our feelings, hopes, points of view, and values, as well as giving expression to our personality and identity.

All this gives rise to literature, to wondrous writings such as epics, poems, stories, and historical narrative. Each of these forms of literature is found in the Bible, considered scripture by Jews, Christians, and to some extent Muslims, the three monotheistic faiths also known as the Abrahamic traditions. While Jews, Christians, and Muslims might disagree on the number of books in the Bible and on how to interpret certain passages of scripture, ultimately they are most divided on the individual doctrines formulated from them. When divisive doctrines are set aside and understood in less sectarian ways, Jews, Christians, Muslims, and other people of faith find much commonality in scripture.

For some time now, scripture has gained a bad name. Think only of how the Bible was used in the American South to justify slavery; or how the Old Testament was used by Afrikaners in South Africa to justify apartheid; or how the world's scriptures are used the world over to justify social caste and gender segregation. Secular opponents of religion claim that scripture breeds violence, sectarianism, and intolerance; that it prevents people from thinking for themselves; leads to prejudice between races, cultures, nations, and religions; and encourages delusion. Racists, terrorists, and bigots use scripture to justify prejudice, supremacy, and physical atrocities;

fundamentalists and other religious purists campaign against the teaching of evolutionary theory because it contradicts a literal reading of the biblical creation story. If religion preaches compassion, why is there so much hatred between people of different faiths? The answer is clear: scripture has become something it was not intended to be. Is it possible to be a believer today when science and rationality have undermined so many biblical teachings?

Because scripture and theology and beliefs based on the Bible have become such explosive issues, it is important to be clear what scripture is and what it is not. For example, it is crucial to note that an exclusively literal interpretation of the Bible is a recent development. Until the nineteenth century, few people imagined that the first chapter of Genesis was a factual account of the origins of life. For centuries, Jews and Christians maintained highly allegorical and inventive ways of reading and understanding scripture, insisting that a wholly literal reading of the Bible was neither possible nor desirable.

The Jewish scriptures and the New Testament both began as oral proclamations, and throughout history, even long after they were committed to writing, there remained a bias against the written word. In the beginning, scriptures were heard in a communal and ritualistic setting; they were not intended for private use or personal study. Such hearers saw scripture as something to approach intuitively rather than rationally. From that beginning, people feared that a written scripture would encourage inflexibility and serve as a mere wooden code. Documents became scripture not, initially, because they were thought to be divinely inspired, but because they provided a sense of community and identity, bringing people together rather than dividing them into sects and denominations. When people approached the Bible intuitively, they found it produced a holistic understanding of reality in which things that seemed separate and even opposite coincided and revealed an unexpected unity, a sense of completeness and oneness.

Scripture is best understood as dialogue, its meaning not limited to what particular individuals say it is, be they religious authorities or scholarly experts. The point of this dialogue is that each reader must interact with the text, personalizing it. The following questions, then, are central to each reading: What do I see in the text? How does a text speak in a given existential moment? In this interaction, we must be careful not to freeze the meaning of a text, thereby reducing it to "dead orthodoxy." What is of ultimate importance, however, is not the text itself, but that it serve as a vehicle or bridge to transcendence, rending readers more loving, compassionate, and caring for their planet and for all of its creatures, great and small.

SCRIPTURE AND TRADITION

The Jewish Bible (known to Christians as the Old Testament) and the Christian New Testament are ancient. Some portions of the Old Testament may have been written around three thousand years ago, while the books of the New Testament are about two thousand years old. In the twenty-first century, why should we study such archaic writings?

Many people, of course, read the Bible as scripture, meaning it is fundamental to their identity. They consider the Bible to be the Word of God and are committed to living their lives on the basis of the values they find therein. They read the Bible weekly in worship and live liturgically, their lives impacted deeply by ritual observances based on stories found in these texts, such as the Jewish Passover and Yom Kippur or the Christian Easter and Christmas.

There are other less religious reasons the Bible should be studied today. These are particularly relevant for readers who have little or no connection with the Bible as sacred text, but are important for those who are guided by its spiritual values and moral teachings. In addition to its spiritual and religious significance, the Bible continues to have a profound cultural influence on the Western world, including artistic, literary, political, and legal influence. The Bible, after all, is great literature, and those who ignore it cannot be considered educated.

The word "Bible" derives from the Greek *biblia*, which means "books." The Bible is not a single book but rather a collection of writings. It is a library of diverse pieces of literature that were collected together as scripture by Jewish and Christian communities. In the ancient world "book" really meant "scroll." With the development of the codex (a book with leaves or pages), a collection of books could be bound together in a single volume, and the Bible represents such a format.

A strong connection exists between "scripture" and "tradition," terms of special significance for scholars and others who think historically. People sometimes question which came first, scripture or tradition, but of course, such a question is misleading, for tradition creates scripture. Scripture is itself a process of identity, and hence, a part of tradition. The history of Judaism portrayed in the Hebrew Bible and the history of the early Christian community preserved in the New Testament, a history beginning with creation, Abraham, and Moses and ending with Jesus, Paul, and consummation is a vividly imagined interpretation of the past that has profoundly impacted generations of believers. It should not, however, be seen as a historical record of events from the past. Through its accounts and stories, successive generations of Jews and Christians have found in it the meaning of their own existence in relation to God, others, and the created order.

Because of the literalist reading of scripture by many modern believers, a process both divisive and misleading at best, we begin with a definition of scripture. By scripture we mean a book or a collection of books preserved by religious communities as authoritative sources of teaching or worship. The main point to remember about scriptures is that they are historical objects crafted in human cultures. The texts are preserved by human memory and recorded in human languages, even if they are believed to have come to humans by revelation. Scriptures enjoy special prestige as "holy" or "sacred" texts only because human communities have at some point agreed to treat them in certain ways. Any text regarded as scripture came to be so because a community, formally or informally, so decided. The process that led to authoritative designation is called "canonical," meaning "rule of authority." This decision to accept a text as canonical is often a source of conflict, as different segments of a larger community might dispute whether a particular writing is truly authoritative for all members. Thus it often happens that a text considered as scripture in one community is simply a book in another.

Scripture and tradition, then, are intertwined realities, two sides of a coin. A "canon," or closed collection of scripture, is also a tradition, passed on as a unique and unchangeable record of communal memory, belief, and discipline. Once a traditional literary work becomes scripture, it is usually preserved in a fixed text that cannot be changed or emended. As scriptures are handed on from generation to generation, they must be interpreted so that the unchangeable text continues to remain meaningful to those who revere it. Unfamiliar words cannot be replaced with more up-to-date terms; rather, they must be defined. Obscure concepts or morally troubling events cannot be revised to suit contemporary values; rather, they must be explained. In most cases, translations must be made for those who are unfamiliar with the original language of the scriptural texts. All of this work of transmitting the meaning of scriptures is also tradition—the tradition of interpretation.

The decision to regard a text as scripture invariably brings into play the term tradition. Most simply, tradition means "that which has been handed down from the past." Tradition sustains a book in the life of a religious community long enough for it to acquire the status of scripture. Relatively few examples of writings penned by a known author have attained scriptural authority in that person's own lifetime. Once a traditional literary work becomes scripture, it is usually preserved in a fixed text not to be modified or emended. Scripture and tradition, to summarize, are intertwined realities. Scripture is the collective term for literary traditions that enjoy the veneration of a specific community.

For two thousand years the Bible, in part or in whole, has been viewed as sacred by generations of believers. At the time of their composition, however, the books of the Bible were not considered to be part of scripture. Rather, the various parts of the Bible became sacred through canonization, a process that took several centuries. For Christians, the status of the Bible as sacred scripture means it is the primary collection of writings they know, definitive for faith and practice. The sacredness of scripture is validated by its ability to inspire believers in every age, thereby authenticating its enduring message.

THE JEWISH AND CHRISTIAN SCRIPTURES: AN OVERVIEW

The Jewish Bible (known as the Hebrew scriptures or to Jews simply as Tanakh) and the Christian Old Testament are similar but not identical. For the Jewish community, the Bible is composed of twenty-four books divided into three sections: Torah (Law), Nebiim (Prophets), and Kethubim (Writings). While these books, written almost entirely in Hebrew, are fundamentally the same as the Christian Old Testament, the arrangement differs. To understand the Hebrew Bible, imagine three concentric circles. The inner circle, the Torah, presents the basic story of the people and includes laws for everyday life. The next circle, the Prophets, is a commentary on the life of the people to whom the Torah is given. The outer circle, the Writings, is a diverse collection that extends outward from Israel's worship and festivals to wisdom reflection.

A Bible for Today

The Christian Bible, after the first five books (known as the Books of Moses or the Pentateuch), displays a different order and adds up differently, making thirty-nine distinct books, in contrast to the twenty-four of the Tanakh. The differences are partly accounted for by the fact that the early Christians were a Greek-speaking community who read the Hebrew Bible in Greek, particularly in a translation begun in the third century BCE called the Septuagint. The Septuagint placed the prophetic writings last, while the Hebrew Bible concludes with the Writings (ending with 1–2 Chronicles). Traditionally, Christians prefer the Greek order because the prophetic books look ahead to a new beginning for Israel, creating a more effective transition to the New Testament. In addition, these books provide a prophetic bridge between the testaments, directly connecting Old Testament prophecy with New Testament fulfillment. For example, Matthew's opening narrative regularly references how the birth of Jesus fulfills Old Testament prophecy: "All this took place to fulfill what had been spoken by the Lord through the prophet" (Matt 1:22; see also 2:5, 15, 17, 23). The Septuagint also includes a number of works that are not part of the Hebrew Bible, though these works once enjoyed considerable favor in Jewish circles.

Some Christian churches, including Roman Catholic, Eastern Orthodox, and a few Protestant groups, add six or seven additional books (plus additions to existing books) to the twenty-four books of the Tanakh. These additional works are called "deuterocanonical" (lit. "second canon," meaning that they came into the biblical canon at a later time than the books of the Hebrew Bible) by these groups and the "Apocrypha" by most Protestant groups, whose Old Testament has the same books as the Tanakh, although arranged somewhat differently. The following table illustrates these differences.

The Hebrew Bible (Tanakh)

The Torah (five books): Genesis, Exodus, Leviticus, Numbers, Deuteronomy

The Prophets (eight books):

- Former Prophets: Joshua, Judges, Samuel (counts as one book), Kings (counts as one book)
- Latter Prophets: Isaiah, Jeremiah, Ezekiel, the Twelve (counts as one book: Hosea, Joel, Amos, Obadiah, Jonah, Micah, Nahum, Habakkuk, Zephaniah, Haggai, Zechariah, Malachi)

The Writings (eleven books): Job, Psalms, Proverbs, Ruth, Song of Songs (also known as Song of Solomon), Ecclesiastes, Lamentations, Esther, Daniel, Ezra-Nehemiah (counts as one book), Chronicles (counts as one book)

The Christian Old Testament

The Pentateuch: (five books): Genesis, Exodus, Leviticus, Numbers, Deuteronomy

Historical Books (twelve books): Joshua, Judges, Ruth, 1 and 2 Samuel, 1 and 2 Kings, 1 and 2 Chronicles, Ezra, Nehemiah, Esther

Poetry and Wisdom Books (five books): Job, Psalms, Proverbs, Ecclesiastes, Song of Solomon

Prophetic Books (seventeen books)

- Major Prophets: Isaiah, Jeremiah, Lamentations, Ezekiel, Daniel
- Minor Prophets: Hosea, Joel, Amos, Obadiah, Jonah, Micah, Nahum, Habakkuk, Zephaniah, Haggai, Zechariah, Malachi

The Deuterocanonical (or Apocryphal) Books

Historical Books: Tobit, Judith, Additions to Esther; 1 and 2 Maccabees

Poetry and Wisdom: Wisdom of Solomon, Ecclesiasticus

Prophets: Additions to Daniel

The first fourteen books of the Old Testament (the first ten books of the Tanakh) have a narrative framework, recounting a story that begins with the creation of the heavens and the earth by God in Genesis and continues with the formation and flourishing of the nation Israel, and concludes with the chaos of the destruction of ancient Israel. The Pentateuch begins with prehistory (Genesis 1–11), including accounts of cosmic origins, the first humans, a disastrous flood, restoration after the flood, and the spread of humanity. The central historical narrative features ancestral stories (Genesis 12–50), beginning with the journey of Abraham and Sarah to the land of Canaan and eventually into Egypt, where they become slaves to Pharaoh. Eventually Moses leads the Israelites out of Egypt (Exodus 1–18), climaxing in a dramatic encounter with God at Mount Sinai, where they enter into a covenant with Yahweh (Exodus 19:1—Numbers 10:10). At the end of a forty-year sojourn through the wilderness, the tribes of Israel stand on the east bank of the Jordan River, ready to enter the land of promise. The account of wandering is accompanied by extensive ritual and legal legislation (such as the Book of the Covenant in Exodus 20:22—23:33 and the Holiness Code in Leviticus 17–26).

The final book of the Torah (Deuteronomy) marks a transition to the next section of the Bible (known as the Historical Books or to Jews as the Former Prophets), as Moses recounts to the people the journey on which God has led them, exhorts them to keep the law given by God, and prepares them for life in the land they are about to enter.

The Historical Books recount the dramatic story of the conquest and settling of the land of Canaan by the tribes of Israel under the leadership of Joshua (Joshua 1–Judges 2); the exploits of leaders known as judges who emerge to defend the tribes when they are threatened (Judges 3–21); the capture of Jerusalem and the creation of the nation of Israel under King David and his son Solomon, the building of the temple in Jerusalem, the division of the nation into the kingdoms of Israel (in the North) and Judah (in the South), and finally the conquest of the two kingdoms by the Assyrian and Babylonian empires, culminating in the destruction of the temple and the beginning of the exile in Babylon (1 and 2 Samuel, 1 and 2 Kings). The story throughout the Historical Books is told from the perspective introduced in the book of Deuteronomy, that the nation prospers when leaders and people are faithful to the law God revealed to them at Sinai. Hence, scholars often call this section the Deuteronomistic History.

In the Jewish canon narrative books are treated as prophecy because they are said to contain accurate and reliable lessons about history. A prophet, in Israel's religious tradition, was not a predictor of the future, but a reader of the present. That is to say, a prophet was one who could look at society critically and discern the will of God for the present time, then speak that will to the people. The authors of these Historical Books were prophets in this sense. They looked at Hebrew society of their time and judged that a particular lesson from Israel's history was needed to insure God's blessing.

The books of the Latter Prophets include collections of oracles and writings of the prophets, usually in poetic form, as well as stories about the prophets. The first three are called the major prophets because they are longer in length, while the shortest are called minor prophets.

The Bible: Its Nature and Composition

The remaining books, a diverse collection of literature known as the Writings in the Tanakh, include religious poetry (Psalms and Lamentations), love poetry (Song of Songs), conventional wisdom sayings (Proverbs), and skeptical wisdom (Ecclesiastes and Job). In addition, the Writings include a group of historical writings (Ezra, Nehemiah, and 1 and 2 Chronicles), called by scholars the Chronicler's History. These books revisit the story of the formation and collapse of the nation Israel, already introduced in the Former Prophets, and extends it to the return following the Babylonian exile, focusing on the rebuilding of the Jerusalem temple, the walls of the city, and the renewal of the covenant with God. The Writings also include Ruth and Esther, short stories about heroic women who play crucial roles in the life of Israel. In Jewish tradition, five of the books in the Writings (Ruth, Esther, Song of Songs, Ecclesiastes, and Lamentations) are grouped together as the Megilloth or festival scrolls and assigned to be read at specific religious holidays.

Daniel, the remaining book in the Writings, is the only fully apocalyptic book in the Tanakh. It includes visions of a dramatic time in history known as the Maccabean period and hopes for a new age, the kingdom of God. In the Christian Old Testament this book is included with the prophetic books.

The deuterocanonical (or apocryphal) books reflect the same literary variety as the Old Testament. Tobit and Judith are short stories, recounting the exploits of heroic figures. Maccabees extends the historical narrative begun in the Historical Books. Edifying tales (Susanna and Bel and the Dragon) and poems (The Prayer of Azariah and the Song of the Three Men) are added to Daniel in the Deuterocanon.

An offshoot of Judaism, the early Christian community added twenty-seven early Christian writings to the Jewish Bible, which they formerly called simply "scripture." The addition became known as the New Testament. Considerably shorter than the Old Testament and written entirely in Greek, the New Testament can be grouped into five divisions, as the following chart shows.

The New Testament

Gospels (four books): Matthew, Mark, Luke, John

Historical (one book): Acts

Epistles (Letters) of Paul (thirteen books): Romans, 1 and 2 Corinthians, Galatians, Ephesians, Philippians, Colossians, 1 and 2 Thessalonians, 1 and 2 Timothy, Titus, Philemon

General (Catholic) Epistles (eight books): Hebrews, James, 1 and 2 Peter, 1, 2, and 3 John, Jude

Prophetic (1 book): Revelation

The books of the New Testament are not arranged according to chronology, that is, according to the order in which they were written, but rather according to the order in which the material they report happened.

- Gospels – deal with the life of Jesus
- Acts – deals with the birth of the church
- Epistles of Paul – deal with the growth of the church
- General Epistles – deal with the general nature of the church
- Revelation – deals with the immediate and distant future of the church

The New Testament begins with four works known as gospels. Each is a narrative of the life and teachings of Jesus of Nazareth, proclaiming him to be the Christ, which means the Messiah, the one anointed by God to fulfill the promises made to Israel. What began as a largely oral tradition, handed down in no particular order, gradually became a set of texts. The first three gospels, similar in structure and content, are known collectively as the Synoptics, whereas John, the last to be written and distinct in structure and point of view, is known as the Fourth Gospel.

The gospels are followed in the New Testament by Acts of the Apostles, a historical narrative that recounts a geographic shift—the spread of the Christian message from Jerusalem to Rome—and an ethnic shift—from a church predominantly Jewish to one predominantly Gentile in nature. Acts focuses on the role of two prominent individuals: Peter, an apostle of Jesus, and Paul, commissioned apostle by the risen Christ. Modern scholarship supports the view that the gospel of Luke and the Acts of the Apostles share authorship and purpose, joint volumes in a connected historical narrative of the birth of Christianity.

Thirteen of the twenty-seven books of the New Testament are letters attributed to Paul, who helped shape Christian belief, practice, and ethics and was instrumental in the spread of Christianity across the Mediterranean world. Paul's letters typically follow epistolary correspondence common in the Greek-speaking world of the first century. Most of these letters are addressed to Christian communities in the northern Mediterranean world, churches Paul visited during his three missionary journeys. The author gives thanks for the people's faithfulness, chastises them for their failings, exhorts them to live as disciples of Jesus Christ, and clarifies his understanding of the meaning of the Christian gospel.

Like other New Testament documents, the Pauline letters are not arranged chronologically, that is, in the order in which they were written, but rather according to two criteria: length and audience. The first nine letters, written to churches, precede the last four, written to individuals; Romans, the longest letter written to a community, appears first, and Philemon, the shortest letter written to an individual, appears last.

The other New Testament letters, called General or Catholic Epistles because their message is universal and intended for the church at large, are general tracts on Christian themes. The book of Hebrews appears not to be a letter but an early Christian sermon. These epistles are named either for the type of audience (Hebrews) or the claimed author (James; 1 and 2 Peter; 1, 2, and 3 John; Jude). The authors of the letters of James and Jude have been traditionally identified as brothers of Jesus and early Christian leaders. Peter is an apostle of Jesus prominent in the gospels and Acts. It is generally assumed that the "John" of the first epistle is not "the elder" identified in the other two letters of John.

The final book of the New Testament, written by a prophet named John and aptly named the book of Revelation, is, like the Old Testament book of Daniel, an apocalyptic work. It features visions of the end, describing the course of future events leading up to the defeat of evil and, with the triumphant return of Jesus Christ, the beginning of a new age. It is principally concerned with faithfulness, both of Christians and of God.

STORY THEOLOGY

In our effort to see the significance of scripture, we are greatly aided by a relatively recent emphasis in biblical and theological scholarship. In the 1970s and 1980s, a movement known as story theology called attention to the centrality of "story" in Jewish and Christian scriptures.[1] This theme can be seen in three features of the Bible: (1) the narrative framework of the Bible as a whole, which on a grand scale can be considered as a single

---

1. The following is adapted from Borg, *Meeting Jesus Again*, 119–37.

story beginning with paradise lost in the opening chapters of Genesis and concluding with the vision of paradise restored in the book of Revelation; (2) the presence of literally hundreds of individual stories in the Bible; and finally, (3) the centrality in scripture of a small number of "macro-stories"—the primary sources of the religious imagination and life of ancient Israel and the early Christian community.

Story theology not only emphasizes the centrality of story in the biblical tradition, but also criticizes much of Christian theology and modern historical scholarship for having obscured this feature. Theology has typically focused on extracting a core of meaning from a story, which is then expressed conceptually. The story as story is lost. Modern historical study of the Bible has also deemphasized the story, either by searching for the underlying history or by an analytical approach that often loses the story by focusing on its fragments. In both cases, the story as story disappears.

Story theology seeks to recapture the narrative character of scripture. Though it is a recent movement, its approach is very ancient, for the Bible largely originated in story. The story of Israel originated in and was carried by storytelling, as were the gospels, their traditions about Jesus having been transmitted as stories long before they became texts.

As a genre, religious stories function in a particular way. Unlike religious laws, which address behavior, and unlike theology and doctrine, which address understanding and belief, stories appeal to the imagination. The great stories of the Bible model the religious life. And it is with life, rather than belief, that we are here concerned.

At the heart of scripture lie three macro-stories that have shaped the Bible as a whole and have imaged our understanding of Jesus and the religious life in a particular way. Two of the stories are grounded in the history of ancient Israel: the story of the exodus from Egypt and the story of the exile and return from Babylon. The third, the priestly story, is grounded in an institution, namely, the temple, priesthood, and sacrifice. As the three formational stories of the Hebrew Bible, they shaped the religious imagination and understanding of both ancient Israel and the early Christian movement.

1. The *exodus story* is essentially a story of bondage, liberation, journey, and destination. For the slaves, life in Egypt is marked by oppression. The story moves through the plagues and the liberation itself, but does not end with leaving Egypt. Liberation frees the people from the lordship of Pharaoh by transporting them to a transitional phase in their journey: the

wilderness sojourn. That phase lasts forty years, but the destination is the Promised Land.

As a story about us, what is it saying? Our problem is that we live in Egypt, the land of bondage. The story images the human condition as bondage and requires us to ask, "To what am I in bondage, and to what are we in bondage?" We are in bondage to cultural messages about success, gender roles, the good life; we are in bondage to voices from our own past, and to addictions of various kinds. The solution, of course, is liberation. But liberation is not the end of the story. Rather, the way out leads to a journey through a wilderness, a place of freedom but also of fear and anxiety. The wilderness is a place of encounter, where we are nourished by the sacred. The journey takes a long time—forty years—a metaphor for a lifetime. Its destination is God, but God is the one who is known on the journey. It is a journey outward as well as inward. Most of us—unless our name is Caleb or Joshua—will die en route to that Promised Land, as did Moses.

2. Like the exodus story, the *story of exile and return* is grounded in a historical experience, when, after Jerusalem was destroyed by Babylon in 587 BC, many of the Jewish survivors were forced into exile in Babylon. There they lived as refugees for some fifty years, separated from their homeland and under oppression. Next to the exodus, this experience was the most important historical event shaping the life and religious imagination of the Jewish people.

What does this image about the human condition tell us? What is life like in exile? It is an experience of separation from all that is familiar and safe. It usually involves powerlessness, marginality, and victimization. Like the metaphor of the exodus story, this story has psychological as well as cultural-political dimensions. It reminds us of the Garden of Eden story in the book of Genesis, since we too live outside the garden, east of Eden. The solution is a journey of return. The story speaks of God aiding and assisting those who undertake the journey (Isa 40:28–31).

3. The third story, the *priestly story*, is grounded in an institution. Within this story, the priest is the mediator who makes us right with God by offering sacrifice on our behalf. Unlike the previous stories, this one leads to a different image of the religious life. It is not primarily a story of bondage, exile, and journey, but a story of sin, guilt, sacrifice, and forgiveness. How does this story image the human condition? We are primarily sinners who have broken God's laws, and who therefore stand guilty before God, the lawgiver and judge.

All three stories shape the message of Jesus, the New Testament, and subsequent Christian theology. In a still-classic work on the atonement, *Christus Victor* (1931), the Swedish theologian Gustaf Aulen identified three main understandings of the death and resurrection of Jesus in the history of Christian theology.

1. The first image understands the central work of Christ as *victory over "the powers"* that hold humans in bondage, including sin, death, and the devil. Like the exodus story, this image sees the human predicament as bondage and the work of Christ as liberation.

2. Aulen calls the second major understanding of the death and resurrection of Christ the "substitutionary" image, which pictures the death of Jesus as a *sacrifice for sin* that makes God's forgiveness possible. This image, associated with the priestly story, did not become dominant in the church until the Middle Ages.

3. A third understanding of Christ's death and resurrection portrays Jesus not as accomplishing something on our behalf or defeating forces of evil, but as *revealing God's love or compassion*. This understanding, with some modification, can be correlated with the exile story, for it is the way of insight or enlightenment which embodies the way of return, a disclosure of the internal spiritual process that brings us into an experiential relationship with the Spirit of God.

All three stories were important for Jesus, the early Christian movement, and subsequent Christian theology, but only one of them—the priestly story—came to dominate the popular understanding of Jesus and the Christian life to the present day. Despite the power and positive meaning in this model, suggestive of Jesus' love and forgiveness, this image, when it becomes isolated from the others or the dominant understanding of religious life, can produce severe distortions: (1) it leads to a static understanding of the Christian life, making it into a repeated vicious cycle of sin, guilt, and forgiveness; (2) it creates a passive understanding of culture and of the Christian life, thereby losing the sense of life as a process of spiritual transformation; (3) it leads to an understanding of Christianity as primarily a religion of the afterlife, emphasizing belief now for the sake of salvation later; (4) it presents God primarily as lawgiver and judge, picturing God's love as conditional and placing grace within a system of requirements; (5) this story has merit when understood metaphorically, but taken literally, it

The Bible: Its Nature and Composition

seems nonsensical; (6) this story works only when people feel guilt, which should not be the central issue in our lives.[2]

The macro-stories, when taken together, are holistic. They share four powerful elements:

- all understand something profound about the human condition, that life involves suffering and alienation;
- all make powerful affirmations about God, portraying God as intimately involved with human life;
- all are stories of hope, new beginnings, and new possibilities; and
- all are stories of a journey. This includes the priestly story, for taken in context with the others, the priestly story means that God accepts us just as we are, whatever our place on the journey.

These stories, all taken from the Hebrew scriptures, have powerful application in Christianity as well. In addition, the New Testament has a journey story of its own, that of discipleship. The initial clue is the meaning of the word "disciple," which does not mean to be "a pupil of a teacher," but rather a "follower after somebody." Discipleship in the New Testament, of course, is a journeying with Jesus. To follow Jesus means being on the road with him; it means undertaking the journey from the life of conventional wisdom to the alternative wisdom of life in the Spirit. Journeying with Jesus can involve denying him, even betraying him. Journeying with Jesus also means to be in a community, to become part of the alternative community of Jesus. And discipleship involves becoming compassionate, compassion being the defining mark of the follower of Jesus. Compassion is the fruit of life in the Spirit and the ethos of the community of Jesus. This understanding, unlike the conventional moralistic images of the Christian life, presents a transformist, dynamic understanding of the Christian life, where everything old passes away and where everything new becomes better (2 Cor 5:17).

THE BIBLE: A NARRATIVE DRAMA IN FIVE ACTS

Since the Jewish and Christian Bibles are not single books but collections of works, they have a variety of themes and conflicting points of view. However, read canonically, the Bible contains a unified story. Biblical theologians

---

2. Borg, *Meeting Jesus Again*, 130–31.

see the Bible as a narrative drama, with God as the main character. While scholars disagree on the number of episodes in the biblical drama or on what to call them, the following headings adequately describe the plot: Creation, Covenant, Christ, Church, and Consummation.

The Bible focuses on the involvement of the Creator of the universe in the unfolding story of life. The book of Genesis begins with the origins of the cosmos and quickly moves to a story revolving around God's special relationship with human beings, particularly with the nation of Israel. It is the story of God's faithfulness and of the fulfillment humans enjoy when they respond with obedience to the way of life to which God calls them. A central theme in the Old Testament is God's special relationship with the people of Israel, founded on God's promise made to a couple named Abraham and Sarah that their descendants would become a great nation, with a land of their own, and that through this nation (which became known as Israel) all the peoples of the earth would be blessed. Because of this special relationship, the people of Israel are expected to follow the path God reveals to them through Torah, God's law given through Moses and reaffirmed by prophets, priests, and kings at various points in the story of the nation. However, Israel's leaders and people fail to keep these expectations and the Old Testament recounts the tragic story of God's judgment as Israel breaks up. Nevertheless, the underlying theme of God's faithfulness reappears in a variety of contexts, such as in Isaiah's Suffering Servant poems (Isa 42:1–4, 49:1–6, 50:4–11, and 52:13—53:12), Jeremiah's promise of a new covenant (Jer 31:31–34), and Daniel's Son of Man vision (Dan 7:13–14). These references would become vital to the fledgling Christian community's self-understanding, creating a sense of hope that all God's promises were being fulfilled in Jesus Christ (see 2 Cor 1:20).

The Christian Bible reorganizes the books of the Tanakh so that the focus is on the hope that God is acting in a new and decisive way to redeem Israel. From that perspective, the New Testament is the story of the church, a "new Israel" that includes not only physical descendants of Abraham but all people who respond faithfully to God's new revelation (Gal 3:6–9; Rom 4:16–25) in Jesus Christ. Therefore, the New Testament begins with the story of the life, death, and resurrection of Jesus in the gospels and follows with the account of the formation of a new community of faith founded on faith in Jesus, through whom all humans are brought back to a right relationship with the Creator. The New Testament ends by looking to the return of Jesus and the creation of a "new heaven and new earth" (Rev 21:1,

The Bible: Its Nature and Composition

5), a consummation in which the harmony God intended at the beginning will finally be realized.

The books of the Old and New Testament constitute the Christian canon, for Christians the authoritative Word of God. The reasons for its authoritative nature and the process of its canonization is explored in the following chapter.

QUESTIONS FOR DISCUSSION AND REFLECTION

Select one or more of the following questions and write your answer(s) in a journal. If you are in a study group, be prepared to share your views with others in the class.

1. In your estimation, why should we read the Bible? Does our motivation matter?

2. What do Christians generally mean when they say that the Bible is "holy"? Does the word "sacred" necessarily imply anything supernatural about the origin or nature of scripture? Explain your answer.

3. In your estimation, should the apocryphal/deuterocanonical books be read as scripture and be included in all Christian Bibles? Explain your answer.

4. Do you agree with the intentions, conclusions, and methodology implied in "story theology"? What weaknesses or problems do you find in such an approach to scripture? What merits or benefits do you find in this approach?

5. What lessons from the Exodus Story can you learn about bondage in your own life? What would liberation from such bondage look and feel like?

6. What lessons from the Story of Exile and Return can you learn about your own human condition? What would return from such exile look and feel like?

7. What lessons from the Priestly Story can you learn about sin and forgiveness in your own life? Identify a particular sin in your life and describe what forgiveness from that sin might look and feel like.

8. Assess the merits of reading the Bible canonically, that is, as having a unified story. Where does Jesus Christ belong in the biblical drama, at the beginning, the middle, the end, or as central to all these periods? Explain your answer.

Chapter 2

SCRIPTURE AS CANONICAL PROCESS

THE CHRISTIAN IDEA OF having written authority for beliefs about God is said to go back to Jesus, who, as a Jew, based his views on the sacred authority of the Hebrew scriptures. While there was not yet, in Jesus' day, a final canon of Jewish scriptures, there existed a widely accepted group of sacred writings based on the Torah, the five books of law attributed to Moses (Genesis, Exodus, Leviticus, Numbers, and Deuteronomy). Eventually there would be a set canon consisting of twenty-four books (or, as numbered in the Christian Old Testament, thirty-nine books), divided into three sections: *Torah* (Law), *Nebi'im* (Prophets), and *Kethubim* (Writings).

By the start of the first century CE, when Christianity emerged, most Jews subscribed to the special authority of the Torah. Not all accepted the authority of the Prophets (for example the Sadducees did not), but most mainline Jews, including the Pharisees, certainly did. Jesus quoted from some of these books, as did Paul and other New Testament authors, so we can assume that all accepted them as authoritative. The third part, the Writings, was not yet completed in the first century, but one of its major components, the book of Psalms, was already in use in synagogue worship. Indeed, this book was so important that the third part of the Jewish canon could be referred to simply as "the Psalms." This usage is found in Luke's gospel, from the late first century, which refers to "the Law of Moses, the Prophets, and the Psalms" (Luke 24:44).

It is no surprise that a faith firmly anchored in the sacred texts of its parent religion would develop scriptures of its own. Christians did develop their own scriptures, but not immediately. The first generation proclaimed its message almost exclusively by word of mouth and saw no pressing need to assemble its own sacred tradition, since it expected Christ to return shortly. As the expected return of Christ was delayed, and as the number of believers continued to expand, the need for written documents became manifest. With the passing of the first generation of Christians, the need arose to preserve those crucial stories and lessons that had given shape to their community; continuity and order were at stake.

Jesus, as a Jewish rabbi, accepted the authority of these sacred scriptures, and he interpreted them for his followers. In other words, Jesus based his teachings on the authority of a sacred text. In the gospels, we find Jesus quoting from these scriptures as divinely revealed authority. For example, when a rich man asks him what he must do to inherit eternal life, Jesus replies, "Keep the commandments." When the young man asks him to be specific, Jesus begins naming them (see Matt 19:16–19). By so doing, Jesus is stating that these commandments, based on scripture, are authoritative for determining how one can be in right standing with God. On another occasion, an expert in the Law comes to Jesus to ask him which commandment is most important, and Jesus responds by quoting scripture. He is not speaking from his own authority, but quoting passages from Leviticus 19 and Deuteronomy 6, accepting scripture as authoritative for how people should live.

It is important to note, however, that Jesus follows up his quotations with interpretation. For example, in Matthew's version of the Sermon on the Mount, Jesus cites scripture repeatedly, saying, "You have heard that it was said," but "I say to you," and then proceeds to give a unique interpretation of that scripture (see Matt 5:21–48). This section, consisting of so-called antithetical sayings, contains not contradictions but rather interpretations of Hebrew Torah. While a literalist might say, "I have not broken the law against murder, adultery, or retaliation," Jesus would reply, "Let's look at the larger context of specific scriptures, and when we do, we realize that anger, insults, and lustful thoughts are on a continuum with laws against murder, adultery, and retaliation, and, in God's sight, their violation. Furthermore, let's look more closely at these laws and their intended meaning. God's laws don't represent lines in the sand. There is always failure and always room for growth and improvement. Therefore, if someone strikes you on the cheek, turn the other also. If someone asks for a favor, be generous by giving her twice as much as she requests. And if the law states, hate your enemy, I say love your enemies, and pray for those who persecute you. In all cases, prefer

Scripture as Canonical Process

mercy to justice." Jesus, then, had scriptures that he believed make clear how one relates to God and others.

After his death, Jesus' followers continued to accept the Hebrew scriptures as authoritative, mostly in their Greek translation (known as the Septuagint), which were read widely by Jews both in Palestine[1] and in the Diaspora,[2] since Hebrew was largely unknown at the time, replaced by Aramaic in Palestine and by Greek in the Hellenic world.

However, for their understanding of Jesus and the new relationship with God that he had taught, his followers began turning to new authorities. Belief was important to them, and since they were exclusivistic, they began by interpreting the Hebrew scriptures messianically and christologically, viewing Jesus as their fulfillment (see 2 Cor 1:20). At the same time, they began taking the words of Jesus authoritatively, as authoritative as the Hebrew scriptures, a phenomenon already present in the New Testament. For example, in 1 Corinthians 7:10, Paul quotes a saying of Jesus as if it were scripture. "To the unmarried," Paul says, "I give this command—not I but the Lord—that the wife should not separate from her husband . . . and that the husband should not divorce his wife." Here Paul gives a commandment—on the par with scripture—given by Jesus, prohibiting divorce (Mark 10:11–12). Likewise, near the end of the first century, a follower of Paul cites two sayings about the importance of paying preachers and teachers, calling both "scriptures" (see 1 Tim 5:18). The first, about not muzzling an ox while it is treading out the grain, comes from Deuteronomy 25:4. The second, "The laborer deserves to be paid," is a quotation from Jesus (Luke 10:7).

Soon thereafter, the writings of Jesus' apostles came to be seen as authoritative, on a part with scripture. The apostle Paul, for example, understood himself to be an authoritative spokesperson for the truth (Gal 1:8–12). Paul's letters, written occasionally to specific congregations and individuals, were reverently saved and shared with Christians in other places. Shortly thereafter they began to assume the authority of scripture, at least among some Christians (2 Pet 3:16). In fact, Paul's authority was becoming so significant that documents written by others were being ascribed to him (see 2 Thess 2:2; also, the Pastoral Epistles and disputed letters like

---

1. Scholars use this term in reference to the "Holy Land," the territories of Galilee, Judea, Samaria, and the Transjordan (the Jewish area east of the Jordan River) in Jesus' day.

2. This term refers to Jewish exiles living outside of Palestine, from biblical times to the present.

Hebrews, which some biblical versions attribute to Paul). Eventually other writings, such as the four canonical gospels; the book of Acts; 1 and 2 Peter; 1, 2, and 3 John; Jude; and the book of Revelation, became viewed as authentic writings of the apostles or their associates, all said to derive from the initial community of Jesus and his immediate followers. In the next century a host of additional gospels, epistles, and apocalypses appeared, vying for authenticity. The author of Luke's gospel openly admits that "many writers" had preceded him in the attempt to "draw up an account of the things that have happened among us" (Luke 1:1).

This movement to consider apostolic writings as sacred authorities makes considerable sense, for Christianity is rooted in the life and teachings of Jesus. However, Jesus left no writing. If he had, they would have become Christian scripture. But since he did not do so, his apostles became the only link to Jesus. If later Christians wanted access to Jesus, they needed to go back through the apostles. This became necessary for each group within early Christianity, whether orthodox or heterodox.[3] Each group claimed its own gospel or set of gospels, and each group established its own claim to apostolic succession, tracing the teachings of its leaders back to the first followers of Jesus. This led to a proliferation of writings in the second century alone, allegedly produced by the apostles themselves but all pseudonymous, that is, forged in the name of an apostle or a group of apostles, some even attributed to female followers of Jesus such as Mary Magdalene.

By the third century, more than twenty gospels were in circulation, all claiming, like the Gospel of Peter or the Gospel of Philip, apostolic derivation. Notable among them was the Gospel of Thomas, consisting exclusively of isolated saying attributed to Jesus. The abundance of gospels was due mostly to the growth of gnostic sects within Christianity, especially in the second century. The vast majority of gnostics were "dualists," believing that human beings were spiritual entities trapped in an evil material world, and that they could be freed, or saved, only through secret knowledge. They shared in common a tendency to produce texts that claimed to distill new revelation. It is no coincidence that the first canonical lists began to appear among orthodox scholars and theologians shortly after the emergence of gnostic sects.

The process that led to the formation of the Christian canon is complex but fascinating. The four gospels now found in the New Testament,

---

3. Instead of the pejorative term "heretical," it is better to call individuals or groups holding alternative views "heterodox," meaning "other belief."

together with the other canonical writings, may have been produced by diverse, even antithetical communities, but all were viewed to be sufficiently orthodox to make the final cut. However, during the second, third, and fourth centuries, Christians continued to debate the acceptability of certain writings. The arguments centered on three criteria:

- *Apostolicity*: the book in question had to have derived from the initial community of Jesus and his disciples.
- *Orthodoxy*; the book in question had to be valued as inspired and revelatory, that is, as derived directly from God and hence harmonious with the rest of the New Testament.
- *Catholicity*; the book in question had to be accepted and used by a wide range of communities, especially those considered authoritative or apostolic.

At first, a local church had only a few apostolic letters and perhaps one or two gospels. During the course of the second century most churches came to possess and acknowledge a canon that included the present four gospels, Acts, thirteen letters attributed to Paul, 1 Peter, and 1 John. Seven books still lacked general recognition: Hebrews, James, 2 Peter, 2 and 3 John, Jude, and Revelation. On the other hand, certain Christian writings, such as the first letter of Clement, the letter of Barnabas, the Shepherd of Hermas, and the Didache, were accepted as authoritative by several ecclesiastical writers, though rejected by the majority.

Paradoxically, Marcion, the second-century heretical Christian preacher, was responsible for the first canon of the New Testament. Unable to reconcile the Old Testament's portrayal of God as violent and vengeful with the New Testament's portrayal of God as good and loving, he created a restrictive canon that excluded all of the Old Testament and any Christian literature that had Jewish overtones. Marcion's teaching prompted a hearing before other clergy in Rome that resulted in his condemnation. Soon afterward, other church leaders began to form their own canon or list of approved books. The most famous of these is the Muratorian Canon, dated to the church at Rome circa 190. It included the four gospels; the Acts of the Apostles; thirteen letters attributed to Paul; Jude; and 1 and 2 John, as well some books later excluded, including the Apocalypse of Peter and the Wisdom of Solomon. What is unusual about the latter is that despite being a Jewish work, written prior to the birth of Christianity (in the first century BCE), it is listed here as a Christian text.

Strangely, the development of a definitive canon of scripture took orthodox Christians nearly four centuries to complete. The earliest surviving list to include all twenty-seven books now known as the New Testament is from the year 367, appearing in an Easter letter written by Athanasius, bishop of Alexandria, to congregations in the eastern section of the church. In the west, the twenty-seven books of the New Testament were accepted at the subsequent councils of Hippo (393) and Carthage (397).

THE CANON WITHIN THE CANON

The historical Jesus, likely minimally literate, had no Bible to study or read individually. In his time it was the synagogue, and more specifically the religious leaders of his community, that interpreted the scripture. Today, most everyone is literate, and most people own Bibles that they hear read in worship or read and study individually and with others. Like the historical Jesus, a modern Jesus would advocate a rich devotional life. In addition, he would encourage his followers to use scripture devotionally and liturgically, that is, studying the Bible individually and with others in order to become adept at interpreting its message for themselves.

For centuries, primal peoples and then Hindus, Buddhists, and eventually Jews, Christians, and Muslims, understood religion as a spiritual discipline. They read their scriptures less as something to be read intellectually and explored exclusively with their minds, but rather as a spiritual process that opened them to transcendence. Because it is necessary for people living in modern multicultural and interreligious societies to read the Bible with an open, progressive, and questioning faith, I suggest that they construct a "canon within the canon," that is, that they look for a biblical concept that is essential for all time.

Fortunately, others have preceded us in that quest. For example, when Jesus was asked to summarize biblical teaching, he pointed to the Golden Rule ("Do unto others as you would have them do unto you") and to the Great Commandment ("Love the Lord your God with all your ability and your neighbor as yourself"). Likewise, the early Christian teacher Paul of Tarsus summarized biblical teaching with the "principle of charity" ("the greatest of all values and ideals is love"), as did the great Christian theologian Augustine of Hippo, who claimed that scripture teaches nothing but love. Rabbi Hillel, a contemporary of Jesus, once summarized the entire Torah (the revealed will of God) with the words: "What is hateful to yourself, do not do to your fellow man. That is the whole of the Torah. The rest is commentary."

When people are attuned, awake, and responsive, reality is often "unveiled" for them, and they are able to hear, see, and understand aspects of their belief system at odds with long-held assumptions. In many cases, people of faith—Christian or otherwise—often become so familiar with the "story" of their faith that a veil is pulled over their eyes, making them unable to experience its transformative power.

Perhaps the most deadening aspect of Christianity is that Christians live with twenty-twenty hindsight. They know the story. They know the plot—how it begins and ends—and who the winners are. However, we are living now at a time of religious change and transformation some would call a paradigm shift. Perhaps there hasn't been an opportunity before for people of faith to open up the core questions again and to ask: What does it mean to believe in God? What do we mean by Christianity? What is the faith filter through which we view truth and reality? What is the lens by which we read and interpret scripture? What do we mean when we profess belief in creation or incarnation? Who is this Master that Christians profess as Lord and Savior?

A TALE OF TWO PARADIGMS

It is no secret that we are living in a time of major change, resulting in monumental religious conflict, chiefly in North American mainline denominations. While there are many ways of being Christian in our day, two paradigms—two overarching interpretive frameworks—may be helpful to describe the current conflict in Christianity. The first, the Precritical Paradigm, has been a common form of Christianity for the past several hundred years. This approach should not be associated with Christianity as a whole, though it remains a major voice, perhaps the majority voice in global Christianity. Its adherents

1. View the Bible as a divine product, as the unique revelation of God.
2. Interpret the Bible literally.
3. Equate faith with belief; the Christian life centered in believing now for the sake of salvation.

4. View the afterlife as central; the Christian life being about requirements and rewards, with the main reward a blessed afterlife.
5. View Christianity as the only true religion, and belief in God, the Bible, and Jesus as the way to heaven.

This paradigm should not be equated with "the Christian tradition," as though it were the dominant or only way of being Christian throughout history. In actuality it is the product of modernity, shaped by the birth of modern science and scientific ways of knowing. Since the Enlightenment of the seventeenth century, modernity has questioned both the divine origin and the literal-factual truth of many parts of the Bible, and the Precritical Paradigm is a response to that modern critique.

A second way of seeing Christianity, the Postcritical Paradigm, has been in existence for over a hundred years and has become an increasingly attractive movement within mainline Protestant denominations and in the Catholic Church. Like the earlier paradigm, its central features are a response to the Enlightenment, only in this case it embraces many Enlightenment ideals, including an appreciation of science, historical scholarship, religious pluralism, and cultural diversity. It also arose out of awareness of how Christianity had contributed to racism, sexism, nationalism, exclusivism, and other harmful ideologies. Its adherents

1. View the Bible as a human response to God.
2. Interpret the Bible historically and metaphorically.
3. View faith relationally rather than dogmatically—faith being the way of the heart, not the way of the head.
4. View the Christian life as one of relationship and transformation. Being Christian is not about meeting requirements for a future reward in an afterlife, and not very much about believing. Rather, the Christian life is about a relationship with God that transforms life in the present.
5. Affirm religious pluralism. This paradigm considers Christianity as one of the world's great enduring religions, as a particular response to the experience of God in our Western cultural stream.

From the perspective of the Postcritical Paradigm, the Precritical Paradigm seems anti-intellectual and rigidly (but selectively) moralistic. Its insistence on biblical literalism seems inadequate, as does its rejection of science whenever it conflicts with literalism. It seems to emphasize individual purity more than compassion and justice. And its exclusivism, its rejection of other religions as inadequate or worse, is objectionable. Can it be that God is known in only one religion—and perhaps only in the "right" form of that religion?[4]

The Postcritical Paradigm, guided by the holistic possibilities found in the dialectical model, places equal importance upon faith (as displayed in religious beliefs and practices, both corporate and private) and reason (as displayed in the disciplines of philosophy, science, religious studies, and other academic subjects) in the quest for knowledge and understanding of reality. It also values the antithetical anthropological perspectives suggested in the opening chapters of the book of Genesis—humans are made "in the image of God" in the first creation account (Genesis 1) and "from the dust of the ground" in the second creation account (Genesis 2)—and the tension created by these competing yet harmonizable views. Dialectical thought is simultaneously God-affirming and world affirming. Advocates of the Postcritical Paradigm need not choose, indeed should not choose, one over the other.

THE BIBLE IN THE POSTCRITICAL PARADIGM

The Bible represents the heart of the Christian tradition, providing Christians their identity, their sacred story. Despite its formational nature, the Bible has become a stumbling block for many Christians today. In particular, many are leaving the church because the Precritical Paradigm's way of reading the Bible—with its emphasis on biblical infallibility, historical factuality, and moral and doctrinal absolutes—ceases to make sense to them.

The Postcritical Paradigm provides an alternative to biblical literalism. Utilizing three adjectives—*historical*, *metaphorical*, and *sacramental*—it describes how scripture should be understood. These three approaches apply as well to the creeds and other normative Christian teachings.[5]

1. To speak of *the Bible as a historical product* is to see that it is a human product, not a divine product. Not "absolute truth" but relatively and culturally conditioned, the Bible uses the language and concepts of the cultures in which it took shape. It tells us how our spiritual ancestors saw things, not how God sees things. The Bible is not verbally inspired, since

---

4. Borg, *Heart of Christianity*, 16.
5. The following points are adapted from Borg, *Heart of Christianity*, 43–60.

the emphasis is not upon words inspired by God but on people moved by their experience of God.

For the Postcritical Paradigm, describing the Bible as sacred scripture and therefore as "holy" is to value the historical process known as canonization. The documents that make up the Bible were not "sacred" when they were written, but over time were declared sacred, meaning that they became the most important documents for that community, providing its foundation and shaping its identity.

2. Much of the language of the Bible is metaphorical: one-third of the Old Testament is poetry or semi-poetical literature. To speak of *the Bible as metaphor* is to emphasize that this language should not be interpreted literally. Metaphor does not mean that the Bible is not true, but rather that it is not primarily concerned with facticity. The Bible does contain history, but even when a text contains historical memory, its meaning is more than (not less than) literal. For example, although the exile in Babylon in the sixth century BCE really happened, the way the story is told gives it a more than historical meaning. It becomes a metaphorical narrative of exile and return, providing images of the human condition and its remedy. In other cases, as the Genesis stories of creation, there may be little or no historical factuality. Though these stories are not literally factual, they are profoundly true.

Because the gospels combine memory and metaphor, some of these accounts, when literalized, become literally incredible. The story of Jesus changing water into wine at the wedding in Cana (John 2:1–11) illustrates the point. A literal reading of the story emphasizes the spectacular event as a sign of Jesus's identity, "proof" that he was divine. A metaphorical reading of this story yields a different meaning. It notes the story's literary context in John's gospel as the opening scene of the public activity of Jesus. It seems to be John's way of saying: "Here in a nutshell is what the story of Jesus is about."

The story begins: "On the third day, there was a wedding." The phrase "on the third day" evokes the Easter story at the end of the gospel. The imagery of a wedding banquet helps us view the ministry of Jesus as a celebration at which the wine never runs out and the best is saved for last. Here we have a pointer to the sacramental nature of the Christian life and to the belief that Jesus is God's best.

A metaphorical reading of the gospels provides rich meaning for Christians in all times and places; a literal reading misses all of this, emphasizing belief in the miraculous elements rather than on its meaning for a life of faith. Metaphorical language is *a way of seeing*. To apply this to the Bible means that in addition to its metaphorical language and metaphorical narratives, the Bible as a whole may be thought of as a "giant" metaphor. "Thus the point is not to believe in the Bible—but to see our lives with God through it."[6]

3. To speak of *the Bible as sacrament* is to say that it mediates the sacred. If a sacrament is a physical vehicle or vessel for the Spirit, the Bible is sacrament in the sense that it is a visible human product whereby God becomes present to us.

For the Postcritical Paradigm, "the Bible—human in origin, sacred in status and function—is both metaphor and sacrament. As metaphor, it is a way of seeing—a way of seeing God and our life with God. As sacrament, it is a way that God speaks to us and comes to us."[7] The Bible is a two-way bridge, a path to the divine and a way to connect to our deepest self. Like a backboard in the game of basketball, scripture is a means to an end, not an end in itself.

THE BIBLE AND FAITH FORMATION

People read the Bible for many reasons: literarily (as great literature), philosophically (as a guide for moral and reflective thought), theologically (as a compendium of truth), or devotionally (as a resource for meditation and a source of comfort). Despite the Bible's widespread scriptural use, most devout people read it only occasionally, and superficially. How people read it is perhaps more important than why they read it. For those who wish to engage with scripture seriously and in depth, I recommend that you find a method of study that works for you, whether individually or with others, and commit to it. Of many valid ways of reading scripture, the following are recommended:

- Reading for *information* – to learn as much as possible about the setting of the authors and their primary audience in order to discover the original meaning of a particular passage of scripture and its potential application.
- Reading for *formation* – to establish one's identity, values, and beliefs in order to live meaningfully, joyously, and securely.

6. Borg, *Heart of Christianity*, 57.
7. Borg, *Heart of Christianity*, 59.

- Reading for *transformation* – to provide resources for developing soulcentrically rather than egocentrically, aligning more deeply with one's powers of nurturing and creating, presence and wonder.

Of course, it is quite possible for these approaches to overlap, due to the complexity of our intellectual, theological, and spiritual needs. It is equally possible that biblical passages convey messages appropriate to our varied abilities and needs. Scripture is multivalent, meaning that it's message allows for multiple interpretations. While one text might strike terror in the heart of an unrepentant person, the same passage might exhort devout believers to greater faithfulness and even greater freedom. When you read any book or section of the Bible, particularly in a group setting, keep in mind the possibility that biblical passages contain multiple messages, depending on one's needs, temperament, and spiritual journey. Scripture, like a good smorgasbord, provides healthy options for different appetites. And you don't always have to eat the same food; sometimes a change of diet can be helpful.

As Paul showed in 1 Corinthians, the important thing is to keep growing spiritually. Paul's concern with the Corinthians was that they were in a state of spiritual immaturity, unable to eat solid food. It takes time—and conscious effort—to grow spiritually, from egocentrism to soulcentrism. How people hear and read scripture (eat spiritually) reflects their spiritual maturity.

Having introduced three ways of reading scripture—for information, formation, and transformation—these can now be correlated with the four stages of faith formation, identified by the theologian Brian McLaren as Simplicity, Complexity, Perplexity, and Harmony.[8] Unlike a ladder, which one climbs rung by rung, faith formation adds new dimensions to what one already is, like a tree adds rings. Hence, formation is central to each stage of faith, the scaffolding for growth. The following terms suggest biblical roles for each stage of faith formation. Like the stages of faith, they are fluid and dynamic in nature, regularly overlapping. Nevertheless, they indicate the central task or role of scripture for each stage:

1. Stage One (Simplicity) – foundation
2. Stage Two (Complexity) – information

---

8. McLaren, *Faith After Doubt*, 41–115. See also Vande Kappelle, *Outgrowing Cultic Christianity*, 22–31, and *Holistic Happiness*, 9–16.

3. Stage Three (Perplexity) – liberation
4. Stage Four Harmony) – transformation

Interestingly, certain books or portions of scripture seem particularly relevant to the task of a particular stage. For example, the books of Genesis, Deuteronomy, Proverbs, the gospel of Mark, the pastoral epistles (1 and 2 Timothy and Titus), and the epistles of Hebrews and James might work well for Stage One Christians. The historical books of Exodus, Joshua, 1 and 2 Samuel, and 1 and 2 Kings in the Old Testament and the gospel of Matthew, the book of Acts, the epistles of 1 Corinthians, 1 Thessalonians, Philippians, and 1 and 2 Peter might be appropriate for Stage Two Christians, while the Old Testament books of Psalms, Job, and Ecclesiastes might be appropriate to Stage Three Christians, and from the New Testament, the gospel of Luke.

Nevertheless, for Stage Four Christians, each book becomes more intriguing and inspiring, and, of course, Jesus looks more brilliant than ever in Stage Four. He seems radiantly different from the Jesus of Stage One and Stage Two preachers, who seem stuck in orthodoxy, resisting the implications of his radical message.

CORE TEACHINGS OF THE BIBLE

In my upper-level class "Global Christianity," generally filled with students minoring in Religious Studies, I ask students to complete an assignment in which they are told to reduce the biblical message to its core principle. As you might imagine, the answers I receive vary greatly, as students focus on their own beliefs and spiritual experiences. Since I would not ask students to answer questions I have not previously wrestled with myself, here is my answer. At the heart of scripture are two central teachings, foundational to Christian faith:

1. The theological core – the existence of a Creator God, whose essence is love, and
2. The anthropological core – that all human beings are made in God's image, meaning that they are capable and responsible to live in love, to enjoy intimacy with God, and to share God's love with all creation.

As key biblical passages indicate, love for God and one's neighbor are core teachings of the Bible. When Jesus was asked to summarize the commandments, he responded without hesitation that this involved loving God with our whole being and loving our neighbor as ourselves (Matt 22:36–40). In Luke's version (Luke 10:25–28), Jesus tells a parable that makes it clear that one's neighbor includes the stranger, the outsider, the outcast, and the unclean. In the Sermon on the Mount, Jesus' classic exposition of ethical teachings, Jesus teaches a way of life that culminates in a call to love the enemy (Matt 5:43). According to Jesus, humans need to love as God loves, with non-discriminatory love.

If that weren't revolutionary enough, we could turn to Paul, the originator of the phrase "faith working through love" (Gal 5:6). When he summarizes what God requires and desires, Paul says nothing about correct belief. Rather, he declares, "For the whole law is summed up in a single commandment, 'You shall love your neighbor as yourself.'" (Gal 5:14). When the author of the epistle of James summarizes the religious task, he states simply, "Religion that is pure and undefiled before God, the Father, is this: to care for orphans and widows in their distress" (1:27). What matters to James centers in caring for people, not confessing beliefs. That is why he goes on to say, "faith without works is dead." Real faith is found not simply in words that express compliance, but in actions that express care. We find the same in the epistles of John. In 1 John 4:7–12, John tells us that "love is from God . . . . for God is love." Then, echoing Jesus' words about the greatest commandment, John continues, "those who do not love a brother or sister whom they have seen, cannot love God whom they have not seen. The commandment we have from him is this: those who love God must love their brothers and sisters also" (1 John 4:20–21).

This emphasis on love is not unique to the Christian scriptures. When Jesus spoke of the great commandment, he was quoting from Deuteronomy 6:5, a text central to Jewish liturgy and life, and from Leviticus 19:18. In Proverbs 17:5 and 19:17, for example, Jews are called to make love central, for the way one treats the poor is the way one treats God. The prophet Hosea echoes this emphasis when he proclaims that God desires compassion, not sacrifice (6:6). Similar teachings are found in the Qur'an and are central to Hinduism, Buddhism, and Sikhism as well.

When Christians think of world religions, they usually think of differences in belief and practice. The deeper question, however, is not whether you are Christian, Buddhist, or atheist, but rather, what kind of Christian, Buddhist, or atheist are you? Are you a believer who puts your distinct beliefs first, or are you a person of faith who puts love first? Are you a believer whose beliefs put you in competition and conflict with people of differing beliefs, or are you a person of faith whose faith moves you toward others with love?

Faith develops organically, not by progressing through stages but by adding new dimensions to older ones. Like a ring on a tree, each new sage includes the previous stage as it transcends it. Thus, a key function of families and communities of faith is to help younger members develop the sequential capacity for dualistic thinking (in Simplicity), pragmatic thinking (in Complexity), critical thinking (in Perplexity), and non-dual seeing (in Harmony). However, in addition to being cumulative, the stages are iterative. After you are in Harmony for a while, Harmony becomes your new Simplicity. And if you live long enough, you will surely face new levels of Complexity, which will lead to a new season of Perplexity, and so on. However, after you cycle through the four stages a few times, you begin to feel that dualism, pragmatism, relativism, and nondual holism have simply become four ways of seeing or four skill sets at your disposal. After a few runs around the spiral, you become less conscious of being "in" only one stage, and instead, you feel you constantly experience all of them. At any point, you can access all the strengths of these stages and fall for any of their temptations.

As learners and seekers develop through the stages of faith, it is imperative that the core teachings of the Bible—particularly that God is love and that humans are to reflect that love—be introduced initially and regularly. Such passages should include 1 Corinthians 13, Matthew 22:36-40, Romans 13:8-10, Galatians 5:1-26, 1 John 4:7-21, and parables of Jesus such as the Parable of the Good Samaritan (Luke 10:25-37) and teachings such as love of enemies in Matthew 5:43.

QUESTIONS FOR DISCUSSION AND REFLECTION

Select one or more of the following questions and write your answer(s) in a journal. If you are in a group study, be prepared to share your answers with those in the group.

1. What role did scripture play in early Christianity? Why? What role does it play in your religious life and practice today? Explain your answer.

2. In your estimation, what is the role of a scriptural canon? Should the biblical canon remain open, like our Constitution, subject to

emendation, or should it remain closed? Since no church body ever determined that the canon should be closed, why has tradition supported a "closed" canon?

3. Of those criteria used by Christians in finalizing their canonical process, which do you find most compelling? Explain your answer.

4. Explain and assess the author's reference to a "canon within the canon." How does establishing such a canon influence one's reading of the Bible?

5. If you were asked to identify your "canon within a canon," what would it be? Explain your answer.

6. In your estimation, what is the fundamental difference between the Precritical and the Postcritical paradigms? Which of these best reflects your perspective? Why?

7. Utilizing the three adjectives implicit in the Postcritical Paradigm's approach to scripture, which one best captures your understanding and view of the Bible? Explain your answer.

8. In this chapter, the author names three (or possibly four) ways of reading scripture. Which of these best describes your reasons for reading the Bible? Explain your answer.

9. In your estimation, what are the core teachings of the Bible? (If possible, limit your list to five or less).

Chapter 3

BIBLICAL INSPIRATION AND INTERPRETATION

CHRISTIANS HAVE ALWAYS AFFIRMED a close relationship between the Bible and God, just as other religions affirm a close connection between the sacred and their holy scriptures. Foundational to reading the Bible is a decision about how to view its origin. Is it a divine product, a human product, or somehow both?

Building on the conviction that divine revelation and man-made religion are fundamentally irreconcilable, many Christians believe that the only choice a person can make about the Bible is to view it either as the infallible, inerrant word of God or as a collection of fairy tales with little or no value for modern people. Since the latter is what unbelievers think, fundamentalist Christians believe they must view the Bible as God's very word of truth, defending it in all respects, even on historical and scientific matters. For many, the Bible's reliability is so critical that they will argue, "If I can't believe the Bible when it speaks about creation or history, then how can I believe it about Jesus Christ and salvation?" To frame the question of the inspiration and authority of the Bible in this manner, however, is to do an injustice to the traditional doctrines of the inspiration and authority of scripture.

Acknowledging the obvious human element in the Bible, modern Christians generally take a both/and stance regarding biblical authorship: the Bible is both divine and human. However, this approach is also problematic. Viewing the Bible as both divine and human leaves us two options. One option is to say that it is all divine and all human. That may sound good, but no one maintains such an unworkable tension. The other, more typical option is to attempt to separate the divine parts from the human parts—as if some come from God and others are human. The parts that come from God are then given greater authority. However, who is to say which parts are divine and which human? The Bible does not come with footnotes that say, "This passage reflects the will of God; the next passage does not." Therefore, those who take the entire Bible as divine are consistent, but they might be consistently wrong.

How, for instance, does one understand the Ten Commandments? Most Christians who think of the Bible as both divine and human would say that the commandments come from God. Does that mean that they are equally authoritative? If so, all Christians should worship God on Saturday, since that is the day clearly in mind as the day of worship. There is biblical evidence that the sanctity of the Sabbath was in effect among the Israelites prior to the revelation of the commandments to Moses on Mount Sinai (cf. Exod 16:22–30). And if the Ten Commandments are divinely inspired, why are they written from a male point of view (for instance, they prohibit coveting your neighbor's wife but say nothing about coveting your neighbor's husband)? Furthermore, the commandments against stealing, adultery, murder, bearing false witness, and so forth are simply rules that make it possible for humans to live together in community. Biblical scholarship affirms that the pattern upon which these commandments are based is a treaty pattern devised by the Hittites, a powerful empire that predated Moses and ended prior to the time of Moses. Divine genius is not required to come up with rules like these. This is not to say that the Ten Commandments are unimportant, but rather that their origin is human.[1]

The perspective I am advocating does not see the Bible in its entirety as divine in origin, or some parts as divine and some as human. Rather, I view the Bible as the product of two faith communities, each responding uniquely to divine revelation. The Bible, therefore, contains ancient Israel's perceptions and misperceptions, just as it contains the early Christian movement's perceptions and misperceptions. Likewise, the gospels, which record the account of Jesus, reflect not static truths but rather changing theological perspectives. Moreover, these texts are not the words of eyewitnesses, as is often claimed, but were shaped by the events of the second half of the first century, perhaps even more dramatically than by the events of the time in which Jesus actually lived.

---

1. Borg, *Reading the Bible*, 26–27.

As important as biblical inspiration is to most Christians, when pressed to define the concept, some might reply with a shrug of the shoulders, others with a vague reference to the divine origin of the Bible, and still others might allude to 2 Timothy 3:16–17: "All scripture is inspired by God and is useful for teaching, for reproof, for correction, and for training in righteousness, so that everyone who belongs to God may be proficient, equipped for every good work." Conservative scholars note that the Greek word translated as "inspired" here literally means "God-breathed," a reference traditionally taken to mean that the authors were directed by God to produce documents that accurately reflected God's message to humanity. While many understand the term inspiration to describe something that happened to the authors, literalists note that this verse bypasses the authors and their humanity, speaking only of the written product as inspired.

Another passage often cited by conservative Christians is 2 Peter 1:20–21: "First of all you must understand this, that no prophecy of scripture is a matter of one's own interpretation, because no prophecy ever came by human will, but men and women moved by the Holy Spirit spoke from God." Verse 21 describes the inspiration process as one in which the human authors were "moved" by the Holy Spirit. In biblical times, the Greek verb used here referred to the moving of a ship's sails by the wind, an apt biblical metaphor for the role of the Holy Spirit.

While such a view of biblical authorship may be inaccurate, having a Bible inspired in this manner is foundational for first half of life living and thinking (that is, for believers concerned with establishing identity, creating boundary markers, and seeking security). The implications of such an inspired Bible for theology are enormous: God exists, God is benevolent, and God communicates directly with us, endowing us with providential resources and values to safeguard our dignity and identity. Those who view scripture this way refer to the Bible as anchor, compass, and shelter in the time of storm. Such inspiration implies biblical reliability, down to tiniest details. Of course, when conservative Christians quote scripture to authenticate its own inspiration, they practice circular reasoning, always questionable.

THEORIES OF INSPIRATION

Christians who look to the Bible as a source of religious teaching or for guidance concerning how to live bring to their reading presuppositions that affect interpretation. These presuppositions influence their understanding of inspiration and the authority of the Bible. Some church traditions say that God is the author of the Bible in the sense that God actually dictated the words of the Bible to human writers who recorded the words verbatim. This approach is called a *literalist view* of inspiration. Other church traditions hold that the human authors of the Bible are real authors in every sense, but that the words of scripture are still somehow what God wanted to communicate to humanity. This approach, called a *contextualist view* of inspiration, allows that God is the author of the Bible without specifying how the Bible is inspired, except to emphasize that the freedom, individuality, and creativity of the human authors are preserved. Of course, actual understandings of inspiration are often subtler and more complex than these approaches might suggest.

This book takes as its starting point an understanding of inspiration that accepts the full and free involvement of the Bible's human authors. This approach is called contextualist because it emphasizes that to understand scripture readers need to take into account the historical, political, cultural, literary, and religious contexts in which the documents were written. This approach is compatible with contemporary historical and literary methods of studying the Bible.

Concerning the authority of the Bible, communities and individuals that hold a contextualist approach to inspiration might say that the Bible is best described as compelling and persuasive. This means that the Bible has authority insofar as it compels us to respond with faith, hope, and love. Further, it does not legislate a particular moral action in response to specific situations, but it provides a series of guidelines upon which Christians can reflect on modern issues and concerns. William Countryman, a theologian and professor of the New Testament, explains the authority of scripture in this way: While the church participated in creating the Bible and acts as its interpreter, the Bible functions as the church's judge, constantly calling it to conversion.[2] Therefore, the authority of the Bible is closely connected to its power to transform.

Biblical scholars suggest three broad possibilities regarding the inspiration of the Bible:

- *verbal inspiration* – the view that every word of the Bible is divinely inspired and therefore inerrant;

---

2. Countryman, *Biblical Authority or Biblical Tyranny?*, 52–57.

- *human response to inspiration* – the view that biblical writers were witnesses to divine revelation; their words and experiences may be human but they serve as vehicles to a higher voice and a deeper reality;
- *inspired imagination* – the view that the Bible is great literature, designed to capture the imagination; though the books of the Bible contain heightened insight, their message is conditioned by historical, sociological, and cultural factors. When the Bible is studied academically, it is this view that scholars espouse.

The first view, simple, clear, and unambiguous, lends itself well to the perspectives and tasks of the first half of life journey; the second and third views to the perspectives and tasks of the second half of life journey (to those who, sensing new spiritual urges and vision, are ready to risk letting go of old patterns and securities for the promise of the future). To these options we add as corollary *inspired process*, the view that scripture requires ongoing interpretation. This assertion, flowing naturally from the preceding options, recognizes that the sacredness of scripture is validated by its ability to inspire Christians in every age. Scripture, defined and finalized by the canonical process, has an open-ended quality in that it is dynamic and alive, thereby extending the revelatory process to the present. Viewing scripture as "inspired process" safeguards the original revelation while authenticating its ongoing meaning.

Most Christians, when they think about biblical inspiration, come to conclusions based on three assumptions: (1) God is the source and origin of scripture; (2) God is truth; and (3) humans can know God's truth. In my opinion, each of these assumptions is flawed and ultimately false. For instance, what do people have in mind when they affirm that all scripture comes from God or somehow reflects God's will? In order to make such affirmations, they are assuming that God is personal as humans are personal.

Of course, there is nothing wrong with personifying God or addressing God as personal, for it is hard to relate to a God that is abstract or impersonal. However, to think of God in personal terms presents insuperable problems, particularly when we take personifications of God literally. For example, when we speak of God's "right" hand, are we saying God is like us, human, and therefore limited to human physicality? Likewise, when we address God as male—or even as female—are we saying God has sex organs? At this point, most of us recognize that when we speak this way, we are thinking metaphorically and not literally. Why, then, when we speak of the Bible as God's Word, do we suddenly think literally, as if God speaks directly to humans, whether verbally or through images or suggestions? Does God have a larynx or a prefrontal cortex?

These problems don't go away when we substitute the Holy Spirit as the agency of inspiration. By so doing, are we saying that God's Spirit can manipulate or override human reason or willpower? If so, we wonder, what other unseen forces exist to control our human impulses? Are humans not free? If we are free, can our freedom be relinquished to unseen powers? If so, how can we know when it is us acting, thinking, and wishing, and not some invisible agent forcing action on our behalf? As you can imagine, similar problems arise when we imagine we can think God's thoughts or conceptualize God's eternal truths.

On the other hand, if the Bible does not reflect God's words or will—whether directly or indirectly—does this nullify the concept of biblical inspiration, or make it irrelevant? To the contrary, this approach makes the concept of inspiration more relevant and understandable and less contentious. By way of analogy, let us think of the United States Constitution. Americans don't consider it inerrant, for it can be amended and updated; and yet it remains authoritative for all citizens of the United States. Like one's national constitution defines what it means to be a citizen, so the Bible defines what it means to be a Christian. It guides the beliefs, values, and behavior of Christians not because it is inerrant, but because it shapes their identity. Its interpretation can—and must—adjust to changing personal, social, and cultural contexts and situations. In this respect, its influence is subjective, not objective. Its subjective nature makes it possible to be quoted affirmatively by people of differing theological persuasions. No matter what institution or communities might claim about its objective meaning and nature, practice shows that scripture is meaningful when it is individually interpreted and subjectively applied.

When scripture works this way, it is true to its origin and nature. As informed Christians now know, the formation of the Bible was gradual, complex, and somewhat haphazard. A close reading of most individual books of the Bible shows that they were composed over time from earlier traditions and authors, in many cases developed from oral accounts. In the transmission of these traditions, a theological meaning became combined with the original historical account, resulting in material that was now primarily theological in meaning. Such accounts were retold for the theological point they helped to make. In the transmission of those traditions as well as in their combination, theological reflection and appropriation continued to occur. The resultant scripture reflects the dynamic process at work in its formation and preservation, initially in the nations of Israel and Judah and later in the communities that shaped early Christianity.

Careful analysis of individual books of the Bible provides clear indication that they were assembled from traditions that had been worked and reworked over time by various authors, editors, and redactors. The book of Judges is a clear example of such a process. From older traditions about various heroes of the tribes of Israel, a recurring pattern was constructed. The theme, that the neglect of the true God has fearsome consequences for God's covenant people, is set out in 2:16–23. There we find a pattern of disobedience, disaster, repentance, and rescue, a cycle repeated seven times throughout the book. From this pattern, evidence emerges that individual tribal stories were collected and arranged to illustrate two truths, the first theological (obedience to God ensures blessing) and the second political (kings ensure stability).

One can observe the same process at work in the book of Exodus, where a series of regulations found in chapters 21 to 23 create two sets of complementary laws. The first set of regulations, tied to cultural stability, reflect traditional values regarding property rights and the status of women and slaves. The second set of regulations, advocating the humane treatment of aliens, widows, orphans, the poor, and domestic animals, transcends traditional societal regulations and locates the basis of society in compassion and mercy. The clash of divine mercy with conventional societal values highlights not a static scripture based on eternal unchanging laws, but rather a process whereby compassion overrides business as usual. The same process is found in Israel's prophetic literature.

In some cases, books were rewritten from other biblical books, produced to support a new theological or political perspective. The books of Chronicles, for example, are a recasting of 1 and 2 Kings, written to emphasize the centrality of the temple in Jerusalem, and to affirm Judah's priority over the northern tribe in religious matters. In a similar way, Matthew and Luke can be viewed as commentaries on Mark's gospel, since they not only add to Mark's content but also reorder and in some cases recast the Markan material. The prophetic books, such as those attributed to Isaiah and Zechariah, consist of collected traditions associated with a given prophet, but often reflecting changing or differing points of view. Likewise, the books associated with Solomon (Proverbs, Ecclesiastes, Song of Songs, and the deuterocanonical Wisdom of Solomon) were produced by sages long after the time of Solomon, and the books in the New Testament bearing the names of Paul, John, James, Jude, or Peter were in some cases produced by later authors who identified with those individuals, or who simply sought authority for their writings of points of view. Such pseudepigraphic writing continued well into the third century CE and even beyond.

As is now clear, biblical authors were by no means enslaved to their tradition. As new situations developed, old traditions were put to new use. For example, the tradition concerning the selection and blessing of Abraham (Gen 12:1–3; 17:1–8), whose descendants became great and possessed the land of Canaan, is cited both in Ezekiel (33:23–29) and in Isaiah (51:1–3), yet for diametrically opposed reasons. While Isaiah reaffirms the promise to Abraham and uses it as the basis for the promise of restoration to the Babylonian exiles, in Ezekiel the promise is denied and the people are told not to cite such traditions as a basis for hope and comfort.

Similarly, Matthew and Luke make different use of Jesus' teachings, such as the parable of the lost sheep. In Matthew, believers are exhorted to make every effort to return errant believers to the church (18:10–17), whereas in Luke the author understands the point to be the need to reach out to sinners and other socially unacceptable non-believers (15:1–10). As is clear from this and other examples, not even the sayings of Jesus were regarded as immutable by the authors of the gospels. Far from having one fixed meaning, the sayings of Jesus were evidently regarded as capable of quite different meanings in different situations, and the authors who collected those traditions used them to make the theological point they thought necessary for their intended audience. If the composition of the gospels proceeded along the lines of collecting and interpreting traditions rather than of accurately narrating the events of Jesus' life, then this emphasizes their purpose to be primarily theological rather than chronological or historiographic.

Using traditions for different purposes than they originally possessed is a feature common to both testaments, and particularly normative when the Old Testament is used in the New. For example, when Paul quotes Deuteronomy 30:12–13 in his effort to show that faith in Christ rather than performance of the Mosaic legislation is now the way God wishes human beings to pursue righteousness, he gives that passage a meaning quite different from that found in its original setting. Instead of using this passage to show, as Deuteronomy does, that the commands of God can be followed naturally, and not through extraordinary means, Paul uses the passage to justify his claim that is is precisely that performance of the law that Christ's coming has rendered useless (Rom 10:5–9).

In using this Old Testament tradition with such freedom, Paul was following previous interpreters, doing nothing different from how earlier biblical authors and compilers used older traditions. As Old and New Testament examples show, finding new meanings in old traditions, even meanings not originally intended, is a scriptural commonplace. Thus, when New Testament authors quote an Old Testament text in a form that differs from the Hebrew original, or when modern readers discern in a text a meaning it may not have carried in its original context, they are doing what the biblical authors did repeatedly in their use of tradition. It is one more example of the dynamic nature of tradition that is evident in the literature that comprises our scriptures.

In this context, the question arises as to whether modern readers of scripture wish to be oriented to the past and the old, or to the future and the new. The way in which the prophets of the Old Testament and the evangelists of the New used the traditions of the past clearly indicates that they followed the latter approach. Evidently, a rigid adherence to the forms that sacred traditions represent is the wrong way to honor the belief in a God who is living, who is God not only of the past but of the present and future as well.

This distinction is essentially the difference between "true" and "false" prophets. In Jeremiah 28, when Hananiah confronts Jeremiah with the message that God would quickly restore Judah, he was citing past examples. Jeremiah, however, was compelled to denounce Hananiah, not because he was citing traditions, but because the traditions he was citing were the wrong ones for the new time. God is doing a new thing, says Jeremiah, and sometimes rigid adherence to the wrong tradition dishonors the God who is living, who is oriented to the future and the new as well as to the past and the old.

The same use of tradition characterized the preaching of Jesus. While quoting the commands of the past, he interprets them in a new way (see Matt 5:27–48). At times, he is also quite willing to contradict tradition (Mark 10:2–9; Luke 5:33–38), exhorting his followers to do likewise. It was precisely faithfulness to holy traditions ot the past that caused Peter to miss the point of a divine directive about what he is now permitted to eat, a command he misunderstood though it was repeated three times (Acts 10:9–17).

Clearly, scripture is a dynamic reality that welcomes new things in new times, and that is therefore not bound blindly to the past. As we have seen, that dynamism is clearly evident in the way in which traditions are used in the various books of the Bible. Traditions can be used in new ways; they can be altered and reformulated, and even contradicted. To lose the dynamic tension in the biblical witness, or to attempt to eliminate it through harmonizing, is precisely to lose the witness of scripture to a dynamic God, who never allows believers to become complacent or to canonize a holy past.

As the evidence presented by scripture indicates, inspiration is best explained as a process in which traditions are formulated and reformulated, interpreted and reinterpreted. Hence, it is in a dynamic way that inspiration is best understood. This recognition will have a profound effect on the way we understand the writings produced by such a process.

INTERPRETING SCRIPTURE

There is no such thing as a noninterpretive reading of the Bible. Literature invites interpretation; significant literature demands it. This is particularly true of scripture, its truth claims fraught with meaning and therefore open to investigation. It can be said that the history of Christian theology is the history of biblical interpretation.

The earliest Christians had no Bibles to study or read individually. It was the church, and more specifically the religious leaders of that community, that interpreted the scriptures. This was so not only because it had been the church and its leaders that had defined which texts were "scriptural," but also because the texts themselves were not intended as much for private reading as for their suitability for liturgical use. If a document was not considered revelatory, it was not to be read in church. Since most Christians were illiterate and copies of the scriptures were rare, the majority of the faithful could only hear scripture read to them in church, almost always as part of the ritual celebration of the Eucharist. It was principally through the mediation of the clergy and in the restricted context of worship that early Christians could approach scripture.

From the earliest days, Christian leaders formulated theories of biblical interpretation. By the fourth century, clearly defined interpretive theories were already widely accepted by Christian leaders, including that scripture contained four levels of meaning: literal (historical and literal level), allegorical (hidden mystical and spiritual truths), tropological (moral lessons), and anagogical (eschatological level, revealing secrets concerning the afterlife and Christ's future kingdom). While allegorical and other levels of interpretation provided Christian theology with flexibility, giving it the capacity to intertwine written and oral traditions and the ability to adapt to ever-changing situations, in the wrong hands it could be abused, leading to heterodox beliefs and practices. From the fifth through sixteenth centuries, scripture remained firmly in the hands of the church elites who had mastered the accepted exegetical methods. Major controversies were addressed by bishops through synods or councils.

The Protestant Reformers of the sixteenth century declared that the church had become corrupt because it had buried the truths of scripture beneath layers of humanly devised traditions. Claiming to base their reforms on scripture, the Reformers encouraged the translation of scripture into the vernacular, a process aided by the invention of the printing press. Martin Luther (1485–1546), a first-generation Reformer, believed that faith and the Holy Spirit's illumination were prerequisites for an interpreter of the Bible. He laid down the foundational premise of the Reformation, the principle of *sola scriptura* (scripture alone), the primacy of scripture above all other authorities. Asserting that the Bible should be viewed differently from other literature, he downplayed dependence on church authorities to understand the Bible. Luther also challenged the prevailing "rule of faith," maintaining that rather than the church determining what the scriptures teach, scripture should determine what the church teaches. He also believed that the Bible is a clear book (the "perspicuity" of scripture), in opposition to medieval dogma that the scriptures are so obscure that only the church can uncover their true meaning. He favored a literal understanding of the text, rather than the allegorical method of interpreting scripture, stressing that the interpreter should consider historical conditions, grammar, and context in the process of exegesis.

Probably the greatest exegete of the Reformation was John Calvin (1509–1564), a second-generation reformer. Agreeing in general with the principles articulated by Luther, he too believed that spiritual illumination is necessary and regarded allegorical interpretation as a deceptive device that distorted the clear sense of scripture. Assuming the divine authorship of scripture, he adhered strictly to the principle of harmony, meaning that scripture is its own best interpreter. No passage of scripture should be set up against another; secondary and obscure passages in scripture should always be subject to primary and plain passages. He placed importance on studying the context, grammar, words, and parallel passages, stating that the primary task of an interpreter is to allow the author to speak, rather than to import one's own meaning into the text.

Espousing the priesthood of all believers, the Reformers believed every Christian capable of reading scripture, as guided individually by the Holy Spirit. Rather than leading to unanimity, however, that impetus resulted in further disagreement and fragmentation. Despite their emphasis on scripture as sole authority, the Reformers could not agree with one another on the application of scripture to polity, social issues, and sacramental practices such as baptism or the Eucharist. The unraveling of Christian unity in the sixteenth century led to the emergence of rival communities, each claiming to be the "true" church and to have the correct understanding of scripture.

The Renaissance and the Enlightenment gave rise to ideologies such as humanism, rationalism, skepticism, scientism, and existentialism, each to varying degrees undermining the authority of scripture while simultaneously unleashing a monumental critical effort to ascertain truth in scripture. Searching for truth in scripture, biblical scholars increasingly detected the humanity of the authors who wrote the documents that together constituted the Bible. As Johann Gottfried von Herder argued in the late eighteenth century, the Bible was religious literature, a composite of fact and fiction that was to be analyzed just as one would study any ancient literature. This approach to the Bible came to be known as higher criticism.

With the advent of the modern period, the methodology of biblical interpretation became considerably more complex, reflecting the increased acceptance within academic circles of new methods of interpretation grounded in the assumptions of the Enlightenment. Under the influence of the Enlightenment, four main approaches developed in biblical interpretation.

1. *The rational approach.* Using radical logical criticism, this view regards both Old and New Testaments as resting on a series of supernatural fictions. As such, the supernatural elements of the Bible are not to be taken seriously.

2. *The historical approach.* Treating scripture as an account of Christian origins, this approach attempts to account for the origins of Christianity in purely historical (that is, in secular) terms. Like the rational approach, the historical approach attempts to account for the origins

of Judaism and Christianity in purely rational and nonsupernatural terms.

3. *The sociological approach.* By the 1890s, many liberal scholars had lost interest in matters of Christian doctrine or theology, and began to explore the wider category of "religion" or "religious studies" in general. This opened the way for a sociological approach to biblical interpretation, which treated Christianity as a specific example of the category of religion, itself viewed as an aspect of "social history."

4. *The literary approach.* This approach interprets scripture as literature, attempting to do justice to the distinctly literary categories of scripture, particularly its narrative quality.

During the nineteenth and twentieth centuries, various patterns of response countered biblical criticism. One response was the resurgence of *pietism*, a concerted effort to retreat from the chaos and complexity of modernity to a simpler, less rational approach, where scripture was encountered primarily through one's heart. A second response was that of Protestant *fundamentalism*, which countered modernism by reiterating supernaturalism and the inerrancy of scripture. Fundamentalism was joined by Pentecostalism and evangelicalism, movements that likewise embraced conservative biblicism. A third response, *liberalism*, stressed morality in religion and gave precedence to reason over supernaturalism. Liberalism attempted to redefine Christian tradition in such a way as to engage modernity directly. Embracing the discoveries of higher criticism, liberals replaced literalistic approaches to scripture with moral ones. A fourth response, that of *Roman Catholicism*, accepted religious pluralism and modern biblical criticism while encouraging Catholic laity to engage more directly with scripture, arguing that the Catholic Church was the ultimate interpreter of scripture, with the help of the Holy Spirit.

BIBLICAL INTERPRETATION: A CANON WITHIN THE CANON

In chapter 2 we introduced the idea of "a canon within the canon." For those who find this idea intriguing, it is interesting to note that there are at least four perspectival phases of biblical interpretation, and that within each phase, as the following outline demonstrates, the notion of a canon within the canon changed.

1. Prior to the first common century, the Jews interpreted their scriptures theocentrically and corporately, from the unifying perspective of the priestly community. During the Hebraic, Israelite, and ancient Jewish phase, the canonical core was monotheistic and was corporately implemented across a theocratic society.

2. With the coming of the Christian movement, the followers of Christ interpreted their scriptures ecclesiastically and corporately, from the unifying perspective of the dominant church community. During the apostolic, patristic, and medieval Christian phase, the canonical core was trinitarian and was institutionally implemented across a theocratic society.

3. During the Protestant Reformation and its aftermath, the followers of Christ interpreted their scriptures christologically and separately, from the divisive perspective of the sectarian community. During this phase the canonical core was christological and was denominationally and divisively implemented regionally.

4. During the modern era and its postmodern aftermath, the followers of Jesus interpreted their scriptures rationally, critically, and independently, from the diverse perspective of the autonomous individual. During this phase the canonical core was ethical and egalitarian and was implemented individually across a fragmented society.

Viewed from a historical and panoramic perspective, should the canonical core be theological, christocentric, doctrinal, or ethical? In my thinking, a canonical core appears in Matthew 25:40, when, in his parable of judgment, Jesus informs his audience that when his followers perform deeds of mercy for those in need, they do it unto God. Such a core is unifying because it is theocentric, christocentric, trinitarian, humanitarian, and ethical, yet it is applied individually, compassionately. Such behavior is faith in action, and it is based on a panentheistic view of God, the authority of the Christ, and empowered by the unlimited resources of the divine Spirit.

A METHOD FOR STUDYING THE BIBLE

The Bible, viewed as God's Word, is said to provide us with unchanging values and eternal commandments. As scripture, the Bible holds answers to life's toughest questions: "Where did we come from? "Why are we here?"

and "How will everything end?" Yet the Bible is also a book of bizarre events and strange mysteries, with references to angels and demons, giants and dragons, rivers turning to blood, fire and brimstone raining down on cities, ax-heads floating, people walking on water, and dead people coming back to life.

Also strange are certain commands in the Bible, such as offering animal sacrifices to the Lord, not eating foods like pork and shellfish, not wearing clothing made of more than one material, not tattooing one's body, and doing no work on Saturday. Even in the New Testament people are told to wash one another's feet, to sell everything they have and give the money to the poor, and to pluck out their eye or cut off their hand if they cause you to sin. Women are told to cover their heads with a veil, not to cut their hair or wear pearls or gold jewelry, and to keep quiet in church. Are these cultural matters that no longer apply? If so, what about passages that promote celibacy, discourage marriage, or forbid greed and homosexual behavior? Are these cultural as well? To navigate these challenging waters we need a method (a consistent approach that can be used on any passage), hermeneutical principles, and regular practice. The process of interpreting the Bible involves building a bridge over a chasm. We are separated from the biblical audience by linguistic, historical, social, and cultural gaps, differences that separate us from the text and that often prohibit us from grasping the meaning of the text. To span this chasm we must erect two pylons, one on either side of the gorge. The first pylon represents *the descriptive task* (discerning what a text *meant* to the original audience), and the second pylon represents *the application task* (discerning what a text *means* to me, in my current situation).

The method I use in biblical study and recommend to my students involves three stages: *exegesis* (what a text *meant* to the original audience; in this phase the exegete [the person studying the Bible] is asked to bring out of the text its natural, intended meaning), *synthesis* (where one asks particular questions of the text, gathering and surveying, in an historically integrated form, the fruits of exegesis into a meaningful whole), and *application* (what a text *means* to you the reader and to your religious community).

Step 1: Exegesis

The great Louis Agassiz (1807–1873), the Swiss-born and European-trained zoologist, was well-known for his method of teaching students at

Harvard to observe fish. He left his students in front of their specimens for days and weeks with only one instruction: "Look! Look! Look!" And that's where we begin in our study of scripture, with in-depth observation. This phase, known as the exegetical or descriptive phase, proceeds along three lines, analyzing the text, its context, and the movement of the argument.

Textual analysis recognizes the importance of the original languages, including knowledge of (a) words (their etymology, historical usage, and biblical usage); (b) grammatical structure (for example, ability to identify the subject, object, and the main verb of a sentence, as well as familiarity with tenses); and (c) literary form. The Bible contains a wide array of literary forms, regularly ignored or treated alike by readers. There is a vast difference between Hebrew poetry and the tightly argued epistles of Paul, or between the sweeping narrative of the historical books and the poignant stories of the parables. There is allegory and love poetry, satire and apocalyptic, comedy and tragedy, and much more. The literary form governs the meaning of a passage. If you want to grasp the message of the Bible, you must read correctly each genre.

Contextual analysis involves an awareness of context. Each text has four contexts: (a) immediate context (verses that immediately precede and follow the text); (b) specific context (the book in which the passage occurs; this step includes awareness of author, audience, and genre); (c) biblical context (how the passage relates verbally, thematically, and theologically to other biblical passages); and (d) cultural context (this includes awareness of the background and the historical, geographical, social, and political setting of the text).

Lastly, the exegetical process involves *analysis of the movement of the argument*. Here students of the Bible examine the contours of the text under examination, outlining the passage and exploring the immediate context to determine key terms, themes, ideas, and doctrines. Finally, the exegete identifies the key verse or the core concept of the passage, that upon which all else in the passage depends. This part of the process is sometimes difficult and time-consuming, but the results are expansive, informative, and ultimately transformative. From there one can determine the key to the book in which the passage occurs, and perhaps even the key to the New Testament and the Bible as a whole.

Exegesis is only the first step in Bible study method, but it is an absolutely critical step. Taking this step means you are on your way to becoming a biblical scholar.

Step 2: Synthesis

Howard Hendricks, the seminary professor known for his Bible-study method, was once asked to speak at a church. "Preach on anything you want," he was told, "except Ephesians." When he requested an explanation, he was told that their pastor had spent three years preaching on Ephesians, and that he had only recently begun the second chapter. While at lunch with members of the congregation, he asked, "What's the theme of the book of Ephesians?" and they had no idea. They had all kinds of details, but the pastor had never put the data together into a meaningful whole. After three years of teaching, the congregation had not discovered the meaning of Ephesians.[3]

That's what this second stage of biblical interpretation is about. Synthesis is the stage where you reconstruct the meaning of a passage after you have taken it apart to inspect the details. In this phase Bible exegetes consult biblical resources such as concordances,[4] Bible dictionaries, Bible handbooks, atlases, and Bible commentaries, taking the results of exegesis and beginning to construct a meaningful whole.

Following exegesis, Bible students often turn to the twin fields of biblical theology and systematic theology for a more comprehensive understanding of the text and its meaning. Biblical theology attempts to show the development of theological knowledge during the Old and New Testament era. In contrast to biblical theology, systematic theology organizes the biblical data in a logical rather than a historical manner. Systematic theology attempts to place all the information on a given topic (e.g. biblical ethics, the doctrines of God, salvation, or the afterlife) together so that we can understand that topic in its totality. Biblical and systematic theology are complementary fields; together they provide a greater understanding than either does alone.

A third discipline, practical theology, completes the theological task by developing an effective strategy for Christian life and practice that speaks to the contemporary situation. Practical theology culminates in the final stage

---

3. Hendricks, *Living by the Book*, 43.

4. A concordance is like an index to the Bible, alphabetically arranged, with references for where verses appear in the Bible. Some Bibles include a limited concordance at the back. A concordance is like a Google search; it can help you locate a passage if you only know a word or phrase but can't remember its reference. Concordances are also useful in doing word studies.

of the hermeneutical process, the application of exegesis and synthesis to religious experience.

Step 3: Application

Exegesis and Synthesis lead to the critical step of Application. The best place to start is with questions. If you want to understand a biblical text, bombard it with questions. The Bible demands questions because it demands honesty. It might not answer all of your questions, but you need to ask them to determine if they can be answered. The answers to your questions will come from steps 1 and 2. That is why the more time you spend in the descriptive and dialogical process (in exegesis and synthesis), the more authentic and practical will be your results.

As you examine the meaning of the text in your contemporary world, you will be guided by two questions: (a) what does this passage mean to me? (in other words, what does it say to me, how does it work in my life?), and (b) what implications does this passage have for others? In application, we begin with ourselves. If something doesn't work in my life, then what authority do I have to share it with someone else?

QUESTIONS FOR DISCUSSION AND REFLECTION

Select one or more of the following questions and write your answer(s) in a journal. If you are in a group study, be prepared to share your answers with those in the group.

1. Read 2 Timothy 3:16–17. How might this passage be read, interpreted, and applied by Christians currently committed to the perspectives and tasks of first half of life spirituality? (that is, by believers concerned with establishing identity, creating boundary markers, and seeking security). How might this passage be read, interpreted, and applied by Christians currently committed to the perspectives and tasks of second half of life spirituality? (that is, by believers who, sensing new spiritual urges and vision, are ready to risk letting go of old patterns and securities for the promise of the future).

2. Read 2 Peter 1:20–21. How might this passage be read, interpreted, and applied by Christians currently committed to the perspectives and tasks of first half of life spirituality? How might this passage be

read, interpreted, and applied by Christians currently committed to the perspectives and tasks of second half of life spirituality?

3. Assess the merits of viewing scripture as "inspired process." How does this perspective expand your understanding of the Bible?

4. What are the advantages and disadvantages of the idea of a "personal" God?

5. If there is no such thing as a noninterpretive reading of the Bible, what has been your experience with reading and studying the Bible? Do you tend to read for information, for self-understanding, or as a way to relate to God?

6. Of the four major Enlightenment approaches to biblical interpretation mentioned in this chapter, which approach do you find most useful? Why?

7. In your estimation, should the canonical core be theological, christological, doctrinal, or ethical? Explain your answer.

8. Assess the merits of the three-stage method for studying the Bible described at the end of this chapter. How does this method inform or expand your understanding of the role of scripture in one's life?

Chapter 4

BIBLICAL VERSIONS AND TRANSLATIONS

WHEN WE READ SCRIPTURE, we encounter historical, linguistic, social, and cultural gaps between the ancient and modern worlds, barriers we must overcome if we are to understanding the original meaning of the text. In addition, each of us approaches the text with some preunderstanding of the subject. Those who read the Bible only from the perspective of their immediate personal circumstances, who forget that the passage was originally written for someone else, can easily misunderstand what the text says. We all do this on occasion, but some, seemingly unaware, do so to an extreme.

THE BIBLE AS LITERATURE

As we noted earlier, people read the Bible for many reasons: doctrinally, theologically, philosophically, and literarily, and in some cases, for all four reasons. Those who read it comprehensively do so not simply because of its moral teach or its authoritative nature but because it is also great literature. Literature, as all art, is a gift of divine grace, a pathway to mystery. Each literary experience is slightly beyond our horizon of understanding. When literature enhances spirituality, as scripture does, each literary moment keeps us going and growing.

An appreciation for the literary artistry of the Bible began early in the history of Judaism and Christianity, but it reached a high watermark during the era of the Renaissance and Protestant Reformation, when poets and storytellers viewed the Bible as a literary model to be emulated and when interpreters of the Bible became sensitized to its literary style and genres. The idea of the Bible as literature received sporadic attention during the Enlightenment and the modern periods, but its most notable revival began in the late 1960s, when high school and college courses in the Bible as literature became popular.

Aware of the complexity of biblical writing—combining a didactic impulse to teach religious truth with a historical impulse to interpret historical events and an aesthetic impulse to enhance human experience—the literary nature of the Bible can be defined with precision. It is rooted in an awareness of the Bible's reliance on figurative language and rhetorical devices, its impulse to image reality and human experience instead of conveying abstract information, its interest in artistry as something intrinsically valuable, and its stylistic excellence.

To say that the Bible is an imaginative work is to call attention to its capacity to put readers through an experience instead of appealing primarily to a grasp of ideas. Unlike expository or informational writing, which tends toward abstraction and proposition, the truth that literature portrays is primarily truthfulness to human experience in the world. Because literature embodies its meaning in characters, events, and images, it communicates by indirectness, providing example rather than precept. In the Bible we see not only characters and events from the past, but also ourselves. Adam and Eve, Abraham and Sarah, Isaac and Rebekah, Samson and Delilah, David and Bathsheba, Esther, Job, Peter, and Paul, all are paradigms of the human condition as well as figures in religious narrative.

The Bible is a mixture of literary genres such as saga, story, poetry, proverb, parable, prophecy, letter, and apocalypse. Each genre has its own conventions, expectations, and rules of interpretation. A biblical story, for example, is a sequence of events, not a series of ideas. It is structured around a plot, not a logical argument. It communicates by means of setting, character, and event, not proposition. The same holds true for poetry, visionary writing, gospels, and letters. Each must be approached and valued in terms of the literary qualities and conventions it possesses.

Literature is an art form, and one of the criteria by which we classify something as literary is the presence of form and design. The elements of artistic form include pattern, unity, theme and variations, balance, contrast, symmetry, repetition, coherence, and unified progression. When judged by the criterion of beauty, the Bible combines artistic and literary masterpieces.

However, not only individual passages and stories but also entire books of the Bible show evidence of artistic patterning.

The most basic of all artistic principles is unity, and one of the aspects that distinguishes the literary approach to the Bible from other approaches is its unifying patterns and literary wholes. The Bible is unified primarily by its characterization of God as its central character. Hardly anything in the Bible is viewed apart from its relation to God. The Bible is also unified by its religious orientation. Not only is it pervaded by consciousness of the presence of God, but human experience is regularly viewed in a religious and moral light. One result is that the Bible invests human experience with a sense of ultimacy. Life is meaningful because it is lived in intimacy with the divine.

THE TRANSLATION PRINCIPLE

Andrew Walls, perhaps the leading Christian missiologist today, has compared the nature of Christian expansion to that of Islam, the world's other great missionary religion. While both have spread across the globe claiming the allegiance of diverse peoples, Islam has demonstrated more continuity in its expansion and on the whole more success in retaining allegiance. With relatively few exceptions, the areas and peoples that accepted Islam have remained Islamic ever since, whereas the ancient Christian heartland, including Egypt and Syria, is now Islamic, and the European cities once stirred by the preaching of John Knox or John Wesley are now secular, filled with empty pews and abandoned churches. While it is possible to provide social and political explanations for this loss of allegiance, Walls points to an inherent fragility in Christianity itself, a built-in vulnerability that he labels "the translation principle in Christian history."

Unlike Islam, in which the effectual hearing of the Word of Allah (recorded as the Qur'an) occurs essentially through the medium of the Arabic language and through a scripture that cannot be translated, Christianity rests on the opposite premise, on a divine act of translation known as the incarnation: "the Word became flesh and dwelt among us" (John 1:14). In Islamic faith, God speaks to humanity in direct speech, delivered at a chosen time through God's chosen Apostle; such speech is immutable and unalterably fixed in heaven for all time. In prophetic faiths such as Judaism and Islam, God speaks; in the Christian faith, God becomes human. According to Walls, much misunderstanding has occurred due to the assumption that

BIBLICAL VERSIONS AND TRANSLATIONS

the Bible and the Qur'an have analogous status in the respective faiths. In fact, they are not analogous. It would be truer to say that the Qur'an is for Muslims what Christ is for Christians. "Christ, for Christians . . . is the Eternal Word of God; but Christ is Word Translated."[1]

Incarnation is translation. When God in Christ became man, divinity was translated into humanity, as though humanity were a receptor language. Translation, however, is not a precise art but a high risk business. Exact transmission of meaning from one linguistic medium to another is continually hampered by structural and cultural differences. The words of the receptor language are pre-loaded, and meanings in the source language commingle with those of the receptor to create uncharted possibilities.

In the art of translation, another point arises: language is specific to a people or an area. No one speaks "generalized language," for all language is particular. Similarly, when divinity was translated into humanity, divinity did not become generalized humanity. Divinity was embodied in a particular person, in a particular locality, in a particular ethnic group, and at a particular place and time. The translation of God into humanity, whereby the sense and meaning of God was transferred, was effected under very culture-specific conditions.

This built-in vulnerability is engraved into the Christian foundational documents themselves. Whereas Islamic absolutes are fixed in a particular language, and in the conditions of a particular period of human history, the Christian revelation, including the words of Jesus himself, were transmitted not in Hebrew or Aramaic, the languages of first-century Palestinian Jews, but in translated form (Greek) in the earliest documents we have. This fragility is also linked with the essentially vernacular nature of Christian faith. For Christians, the divine Word is translatable, not once and for all, as though the translation could be captured in one time or in one place, but infinitely translatable. As Walls notes, "Christian faith must go on being translated, must continuously enter into vernacular culture and interact with it, or it withers and fades."[2] Bible translation as a process is thus both a reflection of the central act on which the Christian faith depends and of the commission that Jesus gave his disciples: "Go and make disciples of all nations" (Matt 28:19).

As Christian faith is about translation, it is also about conversion. There is a real parallel between these processes. Translation involves the

---

1. Walls, *Missionary Movement in Christian History*, 27.
2. Walls, *Cross-Cultural Process in Christian History*, 29.

attempt to express the meaning of the source within the resources and working system of the receptor language. Something new is brought into the pre-existent language and its conventions. In translation, the original language and its system is effectively expanded, put to new use; but the translated element from the source language has also been expanded in translation. The receptor language has a dynamic of its own and takes the new material to realms never touched in the source language.

Similarly, conversion takes existing structures and turns them to new directions. Conversion is not the substitution of something new for something old or the addition of something new to something old. Rather it is the re-orientation of every aspect of humanity—culture-specific humanity—to God. By nature, then, conversion is not a single act in time, but a process. It has a beginning, but we cannot presume to posit its end. Translation, whether of the Bible to other languages, or of Christianity to other cultures and mindsets, is also a process, with a beginning but no end. Christian diversity is the necessary product of the incarnation.

Unlike Islam, whose Arabic absolutes provide cultural norms that apply across the Islamic world, Christian faith is repeatedly coming into creative interaction with new cultures, traditions, and different systems of thought. That means that Christianity's profoundest expressions are often local, vernacular, and temporal.

ANCIENT VERSIONS AND TRANSLATIONS OF THE BIBLE

As the product of two ancient faith traditions, one Jewish and the other an offshoot of Judaism that soon spread into the Greco-Roman world, the Bible was first written in the languages of those times and places. The Hebrew Bible, written for a Jewish audience, was composed mostly in Hebrew, though portions of several books were composed in Aramaic, a language similar to Hebrew and common to Palestinian Jews during the exilic and postexilic periods, when Hebrew went into disuse. Likewise, the New Testament was written for Greek speaking Christians in koine Greek (the common dialect of Greek spoken during Hellenistic times).

After the Babylonian exile, the practice arose among Jews living in Palestine and elsewhere in the Near East of accompanying the public reading of the Hebrew scriptures in the synagogue with an oral paraphrase in the Aramaic vernacular for the benefit of a growing number of Jews who were no longer familiar with their ancestral tongue, having had adopted Aramaic, the official language of the Persian administration. At first this oral interpretation was a simple paraphrase, but later it became more elaborate until it was reduced to writing. Eventually these Targums (the Aramaic word "targum" means "translation" or "interpretation") covered the whole of the Hebrew Bible, with the exception of the books of Ezra, Nehemiah, and Daniel. All translations of the Bible are necessarily interpretive to a degree, but the Targums differ in that they are interpretive by nature, often exceeding the bounds of "translation" or even "paraphrase." There is an extensive literature on the contribution of the Targums to the understanding of the New Testament.

In the postexilic period, when Greek became the language of Jews in the Mediterranean diaspora, it also became necessary to translate the Hebrew scriptures into Greek, and beginning about 250 BCE, the books of the Torah were the first to be translated, in a version called the Septuagint (meaning "seventy"), followed in the next century by the Prophets and Writings. Because the Hebrew canon was partly in flux, the Septuagint contains books and sections of books eventually not included in the Jewish Bible. These books, known as the Apocrypha, include works originally written in Hebrew and other works composed directly in Greek by Hellenistic Jewish writers.

In light of the considerable differences between Greek and Hebrew grammar and vocabulary, the Septuagint was a remarkable achievement. For several centuries it was the biblical text used and expounded by Greek-speaking Jews throughout the Mediterranean. After his death, Jesus' followers continued to accept the Hebrew scriptures as authoritative, mostly in the Septuagint version, which was read widely by Jews both in Palestine and in the Diaspora, since Hebrew was largely unknown at the time, replaced by Aramaic in Palestine and by Greek in the Hellenic world. Thus, the Septuagint became the Bible for the early Christians as well, who came to regard it as authoritative. It is the Septuagint, not the Hebrew Bible, that is quoted by the authors of the New Testament, most of whom did not know Hebrew, but were fluent in Greek. The Septuagint facilitated Jewish and Christian proselytism and has been called one of the most important translations ever made, because through it the Bible first became an essential element of the Western tradition.

The Septuagint was primarily intended for synagogue worship. The aim of its translators was not to produce a work of literary excellence, but one faithful to the original. Because of this, it lacks elegance and unity. Experts note that the translations vary from one book to the next, and sometimes even within a single book. For example, the Pentateuch translation, though idiomatic, is generally faithful and competent. It is not the work of one translator or even of one group of translators, for differences in translational style reveal at least six distinct translations. The translations of the remaining portions of the Septuagint vary in quality and accuracy. Some sections, such as the book of Jeremiah, are considerably shorter than those later used for the authorized Hebrew text (known as the Masoretic Text), suggesting the existence of various competing textual traditions of the biblical texts at this time, an inference later supported by the biblical texts at Qumran, known as the Dead Sea Scrolls and dated to the first centuries BCE and CE.

Due in part to the success of the Septuagint in bringing converts to Christianity, in the second century CE the Jewish authorities abandoned this translation in favor of other translations, more literal and faithful to the Hebrew. Since the Septuagint was used extensively in Christian circles and frequently did not correspond exactly to the later standardized Hebrew text, about 130 CE a recension of the Septuagint made by the Jewish proselyte Aquila replaced the Septuagint as the accepted Greek version of the Hebrew Bible for Jews of the later Roman and Byzantine periods. The Septuagint remains the authoritative biblical text of the Greek Orthodox Church, alongside a Syrian version known as the Peshitta, the authoritative text of the Syrian churches.

Following the Septuagint, the next major translation of the Bible was the Latin Vulgate (the word "Vulgate" means "the common version"), prepared by the monastic scholar Eusebius Hieronymus, known today as Jerome. In 382, Jerome, the most capable biblical scholar then living, received a commission from Pope Damascus I to revise Old Latin versions of the gospel, then in use by the Roman Church. Later, on his own initiative, Jerome extended his work of revision and translation to include most of the Old Testament books. After revising the Psalter and other Old Testament books on the basis of the Septuagint, he came to realize that the best procedure was to translate from the actual Hebrew text. His translation, undertaken between 383 and 404, quickly became the standard version of the Western church. In the course of transmission, scribes often corrupted Jerome's original work, leading to the decision at the Council of Trent (1546) to prepare an official Latin version, which resulted in the Sistine

(Sixtine) Vulgate (issued by Pope Sixtus V in 1590) and then in the Clementine Vulgate (issued by Clement VII in 1592), the official Latin edition until 1979, when the Nova Vulgata was promulgated.

In addition to the translation of the New Testament into Latin and Syriac, other ancient versions include translations into Coptic, Gothic, Ethiopic, Armenian, Georgian, Arabic, and Slavonic. According to the United Bible Societies, the Bible, in whole or in part, has now been translated into 3,324 languages (including a number of sign languages). As of 2020, the full Bible has been translated into 704 languages, the New Testament into an addition 1,551 languages, and biblical passages or stories into 1,160 other languages. According to Wycliffe Bible Translators, as of October 2017 there are some 2,500 languages that have active Bible translation projects, and some 1,636 languages where no work is currently known to be in progress.

ENGLISH VERSIONS OF THE BIBLE

The first English version of the complete Bible appeared in 1382, although Christianity had entered Britain more than a thousand years earlier. While the work of the earliest Christian missionaries there was undoubtedly supported by means of oral paraphrases of the biblical text, much as had occurred with the Targums in the ancient Near East, by 680 there were poetic versions of biblical stories, such as those attributed to Caedmon, the seventh-century cowherd, who set biblical stories in poetic paraphrase, sung to the accompaniment of the harp. However, there was as yet no translation of the Bible into Anglo-Saxon, in part because there were not many who could have read it. By the death of the Venerable Bede in 735, a number of translations of the Psalms were in use, along with translations of the gospels. In the next century King Alfred (848–901) took an active interest in the Bible, causing a translation of the Psalms to be made, and using the Ten Commandments and other sections of the Pentateuch in his code of laws.

With the Norman conquest of England, a new Anglo-Norman vernacular developed with a more sophisticated literature, which by the twelfth and thirteenth centuries came to include versions of the Psalter and a number of passion narratives. In the fourteenth century, the Franciscan emphasis on spirituality gave rise to a demand among lay contemplatives for vernacular scriptures as a guide for private spirituality. This led to the English Psalter of Richard Rolle (1300–1349) and several decades later to the translational work of the Lollard John Wycliffe (1329–1384), who together with colleagues at Oxford finished the New Testament in 1380 and the complete Bible in 1382. The first form of the translation was a quite literal rendering of the Latin Vulgate, though it was soon revised to conform more nearly to idiomatic English usage. Having in mind the purpose of placing the Bible in the hands of lay people, Wycliffe's work of translation was part of a more comprehensive effort to reform the church, which caused him to be called the "Morning Star of the Reformation." In line with his mission, Wycliffe organized the "Poor Priests" or Lollards, who had great success in teaching the Bible and delivering it to lay people.

Sadly, Wycliffe's work was followed in 1407 by Archbishop Arundel's "constitution" condemning the private translation of scripture "into English or any other language," and expressly forbidding the use of any translation associated with Wycliffe, under threat of excommunication. The popularity of the version, however, may be gauged from the fact that nearly 200 copies have survived.

In 1428 Wycliffe's body was exhumed and burned, just as in 1415 his Bible had been consigned to the flames. In spite of the opposition of church and state authorities, Wycliffe's Bible greatly influenced later translations. His translation of the Bible into English would inspire Martin Luther (1483–1546) in Germany and William Tyndale (1494–1536) in England, and it was only a matter of time before lay people would begin reading the scripture in their vernacular language.

For 150 years, Wycliffe's translation enjoyed wide usage and was the only complete English Bible in use. Yet it had its weaknesses. First, it was based on the Latin Vulgate, and made no use of older texts. Also, the Old Testament translation was stiffly literal, and the English it used was becoming archaic.

William Tyndale, the "Father of the English Bible," was educated at Oxford and Cambridge. In the years before his birth, the printing press had been invented and the Turks had driven the Christian Greek and Hebrew scholars of Constantinople into Western Europe, leading to the teaching of Greek and Hebrew in the universities of Europe. It was inevitable that these events, together with the reforming spirit of the sixteenth century, should affect the study of the Bible. At Oxford, Tyndale studied under classical scholars, and at Cambridge he came under the influence of Erasmus, the great New Testament Greek scholar who in 1516 published his epoch-making New Testament in Greek.

Having been ordained, Tyndale became chaplain and teacher in the household of the influential John Walsh, where he got into debates with various clergy and soon met with serious opposition. Unable to receive authorization in England for his New Testament translation, he went to Germany. Forced to flee, he traveled to Worms, where his complete New Testament was published. Tyndale's translation became the first English New Testament translated from the original Greek. A few weeks later, several thousand copies were smuggled into England. Despite opposition, he next began the work of translating the Hebrew Bible into English. While living in Antwerp, he was betrayed by a friend and turned over to the secular authorities for execution. In 1536 he was strangled and burned at the stake as a heretic. His work, however, was not in vain, for the year before his death, a complete English Bible was edited and published on the Continent by Miles Coverdale. His New Testament was essentially a version of Tyndale's, as were portions of the Old Testament. Tyndale's legacy would continue, for fully a third of the King James Version of 1611 would be based on his magnificent achievement.

Shortly thereafter, the first authorized Bible was published, the so-called Thomas Matthew Bible, edited in 1537 by John Rogers, a friend of Tyndale. The New Testament and much of the Old were Tyndale's. In 1539, a revision of the Matthew Bible was published in England, the first translation completely printed there. Known as the Great Bible for its size, the work was begun with the license of the French king, Francis I, at the request of Henry VIII. This Bible was enthusiastically received and went through seven printings. The second edition, often called the Cranmer Bible, appeared with a long preface by Archbishop Cranmer.

In the short reign of Queen Mary Tudor (1553–1558), all printing of English Bibles in England was stopped, and the English Bible was disallowed in church services. Mary was fiercely Roman Catholic, and three hundred Reformers and Bible students were martyred, among them Cranmer and John Rogers. Coverdale managed to escape and wandered across the Continent, eventually settling in Geneva, a free and liberal city where many British scholars had congregated. This was the home of the New Testament scholar Theodore Beza and of John Calvin. A new translation of the Bible was begun, and in 1560 the Geneva Bible was dedicated to Queen Elizabeth (whose reign began in 1558). It was the first English Bible to use chapter and verse numbers. It became immensely popular; over 150 editions were published, and it remained popular for nearly a hundred years.

It was the Bible of Shakespeare and Bunyan, of the pilgrims to the New World and the Mayflower Compact, and of Oliver Cromwell and his army. It was also the first Bible published in Scotland (1579), and was dedicated to James VI, King of Scotland.

On account of the Protestant notes attached to the Geneva Bible, which greatly offended the English bishops, in 1568 a revision of the Great Bible was published, which became known as the Bishops' Bible, due to the great number of bishops on the committee. In 1570, an official order required that the Bishops' Bible be placed in all cathedrals, and so it became the second Authorized Version. Though it ran through twenty editions, it never replaced the Geneva Bible in popular esteem.

While not conceding the right of the laity to read the Bible in the vernacular, Roman Catholic authorities felt the need for an officially approved English version for Catholics, based on the Vulgate. The work of translation, taking place mostly at the English College in Douay, France, was published as the Rheims–Douay (Douai) Version in 1609–1610. After extensive revision in 1749–1752 undertaken under Bishop Challoner of London, this version was authorized for use in the United States in 1810.

THE KING JAMES VERSION AND ITS LEGACY

When King James VI of Scotland ascended to the throne of England in 1603 as James I, there were two competing Bible: the Bishops' Bible, preferred by the church authorities, and the Geneva Bible, the favorite of the people. In 1604, the king approved a call for a new translation to replace the two existing versions. This version, printed without marginal notes, was to be made from the original Hebrew and Greek, A committee of fifty-four learned scholars was divided into six groups, three for the Old Testament, two for the New, and one for the Apocrypha. The new translation, published in 1611, went through several editions, but it would take some forty years before the King James Version (KJV) replaced the Geneva Bible in the affection of the people. But once established, it became *the* Bible of the English-speaking people, and in its various forms and editions it continues to be one of most widely read Bibles in English.

In ensuing years, new translations arose, prompted by the discovery of early manuscripts of the Bible such as Vaticanus, Alexandrinus, and Sinaiticus. On the basis of these discoveries, better reconstructions of the Hebrew and Greek text of the Bible were published, making textual study and revision a necessity. By the end of the nineteenth century the text that underlies the KJV became widely discredited. In 1870, the Church of England authorized a revision of the KJV. The group of fifty scholars did its work carefully, and in the New Testament alone about thirty thousand changes were made, over five thousand of them on the basis of a better Greek text. In 1881 the New Testament portion of the *English Revised Version* (ERV) appeared, and in 1885 the complete version appeared. In 1901 the American version was published, popularly known as the *American Standard Version* (ASV). It removed many archaisms, replaced a large number of obsolete words, and substituted American English terminology for words and expressions peculiarly British.

Within ten years after the ASV was published there was serious talk of a revision. New manuscript finds and developments in the textual criticism of the Bible, not to speak of the faults in the ERV and ASV, helped create the demand for a new version. The American Standard Bible Committee was formed to consider the advisability of revision, and if it were advisable, to propose what principles should govern such a project. After two years of discussion, the committee reached an almost unanimous conclusion favoring revision. By agreement, the task was outlined as revision of the ASV in the light of the KJV, and not an autonomous translation. The New Testament portion of the Revised Standard Version (RSV) was published in 1946, and enjoyed great popularity. The Old Testament was published in 1952 and was equally well received. The RSV Apocrypha followed in 1957. In 1977 an "Expanded Edition" appeared, which included not only the Roman Catholic deuterocanonical books, but also 3 and 4 Maccabees and Psalm 151, thus making it acceptable to Eastern Orthodox churches.

In 1990 the New Revised Standard Version (NRSV) was published, the latest official ongoing version in the Tyndale-King James tradition, and it replaced the RSV as a model of what a revision of an existing translation should be. In matters of text, exegesis, and language it goes a long way toward becoming *the* Bible of English-speaking readers for generations to come. Among its features it dropped archaic terms and obsolete language, including the pronouns and verb forms used in addressing God. With notable success it tackled the difficult task of making the English text inclusive where the original is not exclusive.

The New King James Bible (1982), falsely claiming to be "the first major revision of the KJV since 1876," aims to maintain the supremacy of the KJV as the Bible of conservative Protestants. A recent version claiming to stand in the classic mainstream of English Bible translations is the *English Standard Version* (ESV), published in 2001 by Crossway, a ministry of Good New Publishers. According to the publishers, "the ESV is an 'essentially literal' translation that seeks as far as possible to reproduce the precise wording of the original text and the personal style of each Bible writer." Taking account of differences in grammar, syntax, and idiom between current literary English and the original languages, it seeks a "word-for-word" correspondence with the original text, emphasizing "dynamic equivalence" rather than "essentially literal" meaning of the original. Said to be built upon the Tyndale–King James legacy, it uses the 1971 RSV text as the starting point for its work. With its headings and brief helpful notes, the ESV seems to be a compromise between the RSV and NRSV. Since publication, the ESV has been endorsed by numerous evangelical pastors and theologians.

MODERN VERSIONS IN ENGLISH

Two important translations of the New Testament in the twentieth century are those of J. B. Phillips and William Barclay. As rector of a church in London, Philipps first translated Paul's epistles into modern English under the title *Letters to Young Churches* (1947). Eventually his complete New Testament appeared, *The New Testament in Modern English* (1958). All translations of the Bible into modern English owe a great debt to Phillips. For clarity of thought, vividness of language, and imaginative use of figures, he is unsurpassed. Barclay's *The New Testament: A New Translation* (1968–1969), written by a popular and prolific commentator of books of the Bible, is more traditional in language, but embodies a wealth of scholarship from which all readers can profit.

A landmark in Bible translation was achieved with the publication of the *New English Bible* (NEB; 1961–1970). Representing nearly all major Christian denominations in Great Britain and Ireland, this translation broke completely with the Tyndale–King James tradition. Chaired by the British New Testament scholar, C. H. Dodd, the translators produced an English Bible whose language is fresh and natural, but not informal or undignified. Some of its textual decisions have been criticized as idiosyncratic and its vocabulary as too British for Americans, but overall it may be read with pleasure and profit. A *Revised English Bible* (REV) was published in 1989 with the aim of providing a translation even more faithful and understandable. In textual matters the revision is considerably more conservative than the original NEB.

In 1966 *Good News for Modern Man* (The New Testament in Today's English) was published by the American Bible Society. Its main features were the use of "common language," easily accessible to all who read English, and the systematic application of the principles of "dynamic equivalence" (as opposed to "formal equivalence"). One novel feature of this translation was the imaginative line-drawings by the Swiss artist, Annie Vallotton. The complete *Good News Bible* was published in 1976, with the deuterocanonical books (Apocrypha) added in 1979.

When the RSV was published in 1952, it was received not only with appreciation but also with condemnation by some conservative Protestants. Because of its sponsorship by the National Council of Churches, this Bible was seen by some as tainted by liberal, if not heretical, beliefs. Conservatives felt a strong need for a modern translation that they could trust. Several appeared, among them *The Amplified Bible* (1965) and *The Modern Language Bible* (The New Berkeley Version) in 1969. In 1971 the *New American Standard Bible* was offered, intending to preserve and perpetuate the *American Standard Version* of 1901 as the most faithful Bible translation in English. While these were well received, none achieved the status of the Bible acceptable to a majority of conservative Protestants, most of whom were still using the KJV.

Finally, in 1978, the *New International Version* (NIV) was published, the culmination of a process that had begun in 1956–1957. An intense advertisement campaign focused on the trustworthiness of the translators, all of whom, it was claimed, have "a high view of Scripture," believing that the Bible, in its entirety, "is the Word of God written and is therefore inerrant in the autographs." In its various editions, the NIV is now widely used, bidding to become *the* Bible for those who still view the RSV and other modern translations with suspicion.

In 1983, the New Testament version of the *International Children's Bible* (ICB) was published, followed by the Old Testament version in 1987. A unique aspect of this translation is its accessibility to young readers and those with limited reading skills and vocabulary. Both conservative and evangelical in tone, it is written at a third grade level. A more sophisticated version followed in 1991, geared to a fifth grade reading level. Dubbed the *New Century Version* (NCV), it is also distinguished by its gender-neutral translation policy. The goal of the NCV was to offer a Bible that is clear and easily understood by audiences of all ages and reading levels. The NCV text was paired with notes containing advice on teenage issues to form *The Youth Bible*, an updated version published in 2007. Also available is a New Testament, Psalms, and Proverbs version known as *Clean: A Recovery Companion*.

In the same vein as the NCV is the *New Life Version* (NLV), a simplified English translation by Gleason and Kathryn Ledyard. Using a limited vocabulary of about 850 words, the translation, geared for those who do not speak English fluently, resulted from the Ledyard's missionary work in the Canadian Artic to First Nations populations. The New Testament version, published by Christian Literature International, appeared in 1969 and the complete NLV Bible in 1986. As with many other English translations of the Bible, this version can be accessed online.

Roman Catholics have produced their share of modern translations, perhaps none better than the English version of *La Bible de Jerusalem*, published in 1966 under the title *The Jerusalem Bible*. In 1970 *The New American Bible* was published, the first English Bible translated directly from the original texts by American Catholic scholars. The first step for producing a revision of this translation was taken in 1987 with the publication of the revised edition of the New Testament. Like the Protestant NRSV, one of its main purposes was to eliminate exclusive language in passages that are not exclusive in the original text. Also of significance is the deliberate return to the principle of formal equivalence in translation, in place of dynamic equivalence.

MODERN PARAPHRASED VERSIONS OF THE BIBLE

As we noted in speaking of the Aramaic Targums, paraphrase is a restatement of a text or passage in another form or other work, often to clarify meaning. As applied to Bible translating, a paraphrase usually means a version that alters the cultural and literary setting of the original, sometimes adding or omitting material in order to make the text more intelligible and accessible to intended readers. However, what is sometimes called "paraphrase" in Bible translation is actually a legitimate and necessary device to represent the meaning clearly and faithfully in the target language; as C. H. Dodd noted, the line between translation and paraphrase is a fine one.

The earliest scriptures in English, the oral renditions of Caedmon, were paraphrases. In the sixteenth century, several paraphrases were produced, including an English version of Erasmus's *New Testament Paraphrase* in 1549. In 1653 Henry Hammond, president of Magdalen College, Oxford, produced a paraphrase of the New Testament, which was printed alongside the King James Version.

The most popular English Bible paraphrase of all times is Kenneth N. Taylor's *The Living Bible Paraphrased* (1971). Paraphrases of the biblical texts, responsible made, are a legitimate and useful way of making the text clearer to the reader. Of course, the intended "meaning" of archaic texts such as the Bible is subjective at best. Nevertheless, when paraphrases are produced by translation with a theological bias, as is the case with Taylor's self-declared "rigid evangelical position," the results, however lofty, admirable, or attractive, serve only to confirm the truth of the aphorism, "translators are traitors." In 1996, a revision of the Living Bible appeared as the *New Living Translation* (NLT), essentially a new translation separate from the LB.

Another magnificent paraphrase, published in segments from 1993 to 2002 is pastor, author, and biblical scholar Eugene H. Peterson's work *The Message: The Bible in Contemporary Language*. Intent on sharing the joy and power of the Christian life with others, Peterson found himself translating the Bible for his congregation. A scholar of the Greek and Hebrew languages, Peterson worked to produce a paraphrase of the Bible in the idiom of our day. Not surprisingly, the version reached a wide audience, including many in the artistic community and others taken by its startling vocabulary and familiar style, which, designed to make visible what is invisible, encourages a sense of intimacy with God. Indeed, isn't that what reading the Bible is about, loving God with all our body, mind, heart, and soul, and our neighbor as ourselves?

QUESTIONS FOR DISCUSSION AND REFLECTION

Select one or more of the following questions and write your answer(s) in a journal. If you are in a group study, be prepared to share your answers with those in the group.

1. In your estimation, does conceptualizing the Bible as literature enhance or diminish its meaning and relevance? Explain your answer.
2. What does this chapter say about the "translation principle" in Christianity? What does this chapter say about the differences between

Christianity and Islam regarding Christ and truth? Explain your answer.

3. Explain the significance of the concept of an authorized version of the Bible in England.

4. Explain the popularity of the King James Version of the Bible in the English-speaking world, and the suspicion in the minds of many conservative Protestants regarding any translation departing from its legacy.

5. Explain the faults of the King James Bible and the need for ongoing translations and updated versions of the Bible.

6. Explain the benefits and the faults of paraphrased Bibles.

7. Which version of the Bible do you prefer reading or studying? Explain your answer. If, while reading this chapter, another version got your attention as the version of the Bible or New Testament you would like to read or study next, what is it? Explain your answer.

Chapter 5

OLD TESTAMENT LITERATURE, PART I
Overview and Passages

THIS CHAPTER AND THE next three chapters provide a brief introduction to each book of the Bible in literary sequence (namely, in their biblical order). Chapter 5 provides an introduction to the five books of Mosaic law (called the Torah or Pentateuch), followed by twelve historical books and four poetic and wisdom books, in addition to two apocryphal/deuterocanonical writings (Wisdom of Solomon and Sirach), and concluding with the biblical Song of Songs and the apocryphal (deuterocanonical) book of Tobit. Each introductory overview is followed by a list of recommended readings from that book of the Bible. A complete guide of daily readings, designed to lead individuals through the sixty-six books of the Bible (plus several of the apocryphal/deuterocanonical books) in eleven months or less, is provided in the appendix to this book.

THE PENTATEUCH AND HISTORICAL LITERATURE

Genesis

Introductory Overview

Genesis, meaning "beginnings," recounts the birth of the cosmos, the origin of life on earth, the beginning of civilization, Israel's earliest ancestors, and founding events of religious traditions. Theologically basic to the Old and New Testaments, Genesis contains two major parts: the primeval history (chapters 1–11 and the ancestral history (chapters 12–50). Like the other books of the Pentateuch, Genesis contains writings from multiple authors and sources, including some literary traditions datable to the time of Moses. Central to the account is the covenant-making character of God.

Recommended Readings (passages separated by semicolons indicate chapters; passages separated by colons indicate verses)

Chapters 1–4; 6:1–9:17; 11:1–9; 11:27–25:11; 25:19–34; 27–33; 35; 37; 39–46; 47–50

Exodus

Introductory Overview

Exodus focuses on the role of Moses in arguably the central events in the establishment of Israel as a people: the exodus from Egypt and the institution at Mount Sinai of the covenant between God and Israel. The book contains two major parts: the first relates the story of Moses, the oppression of the Israelites, the establishment of the Passover, and the manner of Israel's deliverance from Egypt (chapter 1–18), and the second relates the account of the covenant regulations by means of which the Israelite community was to govern its life and worship. Focusing on two aspects of the character of God, namely the nature of divine power and of divine presence in the world, the book of Exodus has been a source of inspiration for movements of liberation around the world.

Recommended Readings (passages separated by semicolons indicate chapters; passages separated by colons indicate verses)

Chapters 1:1–4:20; 4:27–6:13; 7:8–12:42; 13:17–25:40; 28:1–4; 31:18–34:35; 40

Leviticus

Introductory Overview

The name Leviticus means "pertaining to the Levites," expressing the fact that much of this book has to do with the laws of worship and purification, for which the priests in ancient Israel, who were of the tribe of Levi, were primarily responsible. Leviticus is part of a longer literary complex of priestly accounts of the origin of the wilderness sanctuary (known as the tabernacle or tent of meeting) and its personnel and rituals that extends from Exodus 25 to Numbers 10. The language and theology of Leviticus are reflected in the words and ideas of certain New Testament writers, notably in the book of Hebrews, where the priesthood of Jesus Christ is contrasted with the Levitical priesthood.

Recommended Readings (passages separated by semicolons indicate chapters; passages separated by colons indicate verses)

Readers are asked to skip the book of Leviticus in its entirety and to proceed to the second half of the book of Numbers.

Numbers

Introductory Overview

Numbers begins with preparations for departure from Mount Sinai and recounts Israel's experience marching through the wilderness for nearly forty years. The book's title derives from the two census lists that forms the book's structure: the first major census list (in chapter 1) describes experiences of the first wilderness generation of Israelites who had experienced the exodus from Egypt and the covenant at Mount Sinai, whereas the second census list (in chapter 26) describes experiences of the new generation of Israelites who will lead the people into the promised land of Canaan. Despite rebellion and disobedience, Israel is guided and sustained in their long and perilous journey by the grace of God, thereby realizing God's ancient promise to the ancestors in the book of Genesis (15:18–21; see also Deut 1:8).

Recommended Readings (passages separated by semicolons indicate chapters; passages separated by colons indicate verses)

Chapters 10:11–14:45; 20–24; 26:63–27:23

Deuteronomy

Introductory Overview

While the title Deuteronomy is the Greek translation of the Hebrew word used in Deuteronomy 17:18 for "a second law," the title does not suggest that the book contains a law different from that given at Mount Sinai.

Instead, the title reapplies the one law to the second wilderness generation facing new circumstances. Insisting that there is but one covenant binding God and the people, Deuteronomy recognizes that each generation must faithfully interpret the principles of the covenantal relation with God in new settings. Repeating much of the legislation found in Exodus, Leviticus, and Numbers, in Deuteronomy Moses delivers three speeches in the plains of Moab as a farewell to his people, exhorting Israel to fidelity in its forthcoming invasion of Canaan.

Recommended Readings (passages separated by semicolons indicate chapters; passages separated by colons indicate verses)

Chapters 1-6; 18:9–22; 27:9–30:20; 34

Joshua

Introductory Overview

Joshua tells the story of the conquest of Canaan and how, with the passing of Moses, Joshua assumes leadership of the Israelites. A sequel to Deuteronomy, Joshua tells how the land is divided among the twelve tribes. Comparison with the book of Judges indicates that the story of the conquest of Canaan is idealized and that the conquest was less decisive and complete than Joshua suggests. A controversial topic in Joshua is its emphasis on holy war. However, the narrative can be read without explicit evidence of widespread genocide. For example, Israel's wars are primarily defensive and while Israel does attack Jericho and Ai, archaeological evidence suggests that these sites were not civilian cities but rather military forts. Of central theological importance throughout the book is obedience to God's instruction, the dangers of division and loss of unity, the land as a gift of God, and the holiness of God.

Recommended Readings (passages separated by semicolons indicate chapters; passages separated by colons indicate verses)

Chapters 1–11; 21:41–24:33

Judges

Introductory Overview

Judges is a composite of independent stories related to the tribal period, which followed the death of Joshua and preceded the unification of the tribes under a single king. The book is a continuation of the Deuteronomistic historical perspective evident in Deuteronomy and Joshua and continuing with Judges, Samuel, Kings, and included in the prophets Hosea and Jeremiah. The final editor, in preserving the tradition of various tribes and the exploits of twelve national or local heroes or military leaders called "judges," was concerned with the moral lesson that loyalty to God brings national success and disloyalty guarantees disaster.

Recommended Readings (passages separated by semicolons indicate chapters; passages separated by colons indicate verses)

Chapters 1–16

Ruth

Introductory Overview

Set in the period of the judges, the book of Ruth tells the story of a Moabite woman who, after the death of her husband, travels with her mother-in-law Naomi to Judah. There, her devotion to Naomi brings Ruth to the attention of Boaz, a relative of her late husband. Boaz marries Ruth and through the marriage she becomes the great-grandmother of King David. The story of Ruth's devotion to Naomi is upheld as a model of true piety. In addition, this book testifies that trust in God will be rewarded and that God's goodness transcends nationalistic boundaries. In the Hebrew Bible this book is placed with the Writings, where it is listed among the five scrolls read at festivals, in this case the Festival of Tabernacles of Weeks celebrated by Christians as Pentecost.

Recommended Readings (passages separated by semicolons indicate chapters; passages separated by colons indicate verses)

A storytelling masterpiece, this book should be read in its entirety.

1 and 2 Samuel

Introductory Overview

Continuing the Deuteronomistic history, 1 and 2 Samuel were originally one book. Though they bear the name of Samuel, he is the focal character only in 1 Samuel 1–8. The main interest of 1 and 2 Samuel is David. First Samuel tells of his rise and 2 Samuel of his kingship. The prophet Samuel introduces monarchy into Israel, and Saul, the first king, is a foil to David. In these books, David is the hero, but a flawed one at best. Nevertheless, he is divinely chosen and prepared for the throne. As so often in the Old Testament, the narrative emphasizes that despite sin and human failing, God's providence accomplishes its intention. In 2 Samuel, the prophecy of Nathan promising David an everlasting dynasty (7:1–17) becomes the basis for the development of royal messianism throughout the Bible. Central to 1 and 2 Samuel is the importance of good government and the difficulty in establishing it. Unlike in the Pentateuch, in 1 and 2 Samuel God tends to move in the background rather than acting on center stage.

Recommended Readings (passages separated by semicolons indicate chapters; passages separated by colons indicate verses)

Because of their fascinating characters, sustained storytelling, and importance for understanding the rest of the Bible, the books of 1 and 2 Samuel should be read in their entirety.

1 and 2 Kings

Introductory Overview

The establishment of David's dynasty and the building of Solomon's temple bring to completion God's work of establishing Israel in Canaan (1 Kgs 1–10). However, Israel's prosperity has a condition, that God's commandments be obeyed. Hence, the rest of 1 and 2 Kings tells how disaster comes to Israel and Judah. Only two kings of Judah, Hezekiah and Josiah, are approved due to consistent faithfulness to the national theocratic obligations. These books also ascribe a dominant role to the prophets Elijah and Elisha and their conflict with King Ahab and his Baal-worshipping queen, Jezebel.

In overt and covert ways, 1 and 2 Kings provide a prophetic interpretation of the 400-year period of the monarchy, from the end of the reign of

David and the ascension of Solomon through the fall of Israel in 721 to the conquest of Judah in 586 BCE. The writers of Kings selected and arranged the written and oral traditions of Israel and Judah to express their theological understanding of these histories. Continuing the Deuteronomistic stress on fidelity to God, 1 and 2 Kings contend that to practice idolatry (worshipping gods other than Yahweh) is to forsake the God of Israel. At many points in the books of Samuel and Kings, prophets arise and the editors pause to pass judgment on the rulers of Israel and Judah in light of their covenant obligations to the God of Israel. Furthermore, since Israel is God's people by covenant, recurring attention is given to the covenant and, because of it, to Israel as God's unique people.

Recommended Readings (passages separated by semicolons indicate chapters; passages separated by colons indicate verses)

1 Kings should be read in its entirety; 2 Kings, chapters 1:1–2:15; 4–13; 17–25

1 and 2 Chronicles

Introductory Overview

The two books of Chronicles, originally a single book, cover the same period of history as 1 and 2 Kings (the Chronicler's history famously omits the reign of Saul and the period of the Northern Kingdom [Israel]). While focusing on the reign of David and the establishment of his dynasty, nothing is said of the faults of David. According to the Chronicler, it was David in Jerusalem and not Moses in the wilderness who founded the true Israel. Primarily concerned with the temple and the worship of God, the Chronicler's history of the monarchy seems to be primarily a history of the establishment and maintenance of the worship of God. Likewise, the function of the people is to provide the necessary funds and personnel for temple services. Some events and personages found in the Deuteronomistic History, such as Elijah and Elisha, are omitted, while other events and a more religious emphasis are added. Because of the Chronicler's concern with genealogies and the role of Levites, it is believed he (or they) may have been a Levitical priest. While the final edition of the Deuteronomistic History is normally dated to the late seventh century (about 600 BCE), the Chronicler's work is post-exilic, and customarily dated to the late fourth century (about 330 BCE).

Recommended Readings (passages separated by semicolons indicate chapters; passages separated by colons indicate verses)

Because of its repetitive nature and cultic focus, readers are asked to skip these books, with the exception of 2 Chronicles 35:20–36:23, which recount the events leading to Josiah's death, the exile to Babylon, and the edict of the Persian king Cyrus (36:22–23) permitting the return of the Jews from exile in Babylon, words repeated at the start of the book of Ezra.

Ezra and Nehemiah

Introductory Overview

The books of Ezra and Nehemiah, which in the Hebrew Bible for a single book, are a continuation of the books of Chronicles, telling about the return of the Jews from exile in Babylon. There seems to have been four stages of the return: (1) a return under Cyrus (about 538 BCE), led by Sheshbazzar, who commenced rebuilding the temple; (2) a return under Darius I (521–485), led by Zerubbabel and Jeshua, who, with encouragement from the prophets Haggai and Zechariah, completed the temple; (3) a group under Artaxerxes I (464–423), which, according to the Chronicler was led by Ezra, who brought a codification of Mosaic law; and 4(4) another group, under Artaxerxes II (404–358), led by Nehemiah, who came twice under Artaxerxes I to build the walls of Jerusalem and to attempt to establish purity of community and worship. Despite the present arrangement of Ezra–Nehemiah, which puts Ezra before Nehemiah, the chronology of events at this time is highly disputed by historians, and this leads to an alternative but highly attractive view that places Ezra's return under Artaxerxes II and after Nehemiah.

Until recently, the great majority of biblical scholars considered the books of Chronicles to form a unity with Ezra–Nehemiah, based on the overlap between 2 Chronicles 36:22–23 and Ezra 1:1–3a and similarities in their theology, a position now in question. In addition, the book of Nehemiah provides first-person memoirs (chapters 1–7; 11–13), a form unique in the Hebrew Bible. The original memoir may have been a report to the Persian king about the rebuilding of the walls of Jerusalem, but in its present state it is an appeal for God to remember Nehemiah's good deeds.

Recommended Readings (passages separated by semicolons indicate chapters; passages separated by colons indicate verses)

Because the texts of Ezra and Nehemiah were distorted in transmission, forcing editorial changes and insertions, the following sequence of readings from Ezra-Nehemiah is recommended: Ezra 1: 1–11; Ezra 3:1–4:5; Ezra 5:1–7:28; 8:15–36; Nehemiah 8:1–18; and Ezra 9:1–10:17. In addition, the following chapters are recommended from Nehemiah: 1–2; 4:1–7:4.

Esther

Introductory Overview

Esther, a story about a Jewish heroine, is set in the Jewish diaspora community in the Persian empire. Similar to the stories of Joseph and Daniel, the book of Esther recounts how a follower of Yahweh achieves great status within a foreign court despite great danger. In this story, Esther becomes a Persian queen and helps her cousin Mordecai rescue the Jews form a genocidal plot. In the Hebrew Bible, Esther is one of the five Megilloth or Scrolls read at great festivals, in this case the festival or Purim or Lots. As this book emphasizes, human action is the key to achieving God's purposes in the world.

Recommended Readings (passages separated by semicolons indicate chapters; passages separated by colons indicate verses)

A storytelling masterpiece like the book of Ruth, this book should be read in its entirety.

THE POETIC AND WISDOM LITERATURE

Job

Introductory Overview

The book of Job examines the age-old problem of a just God allowing righteous and innocent people to suffer. Into the ancient prose folktale regarding the trials of Job, a gifted poet and theologian constructs a lengthy poetic section combining dialogue between Job and four companions about divine justice and human response to affliction. More broadly, the book presents a quest for knowledge about the nature of God and the universe, and the place of humans in it. Containing a great poem about wisdom (chapter 28), the poetic section also includes God's response in chapters 38-41. While the ancient folktale provides a simplistic understanding of the reward/retribution understanding of justice, the poetic section never gives readers a clear answer to the question of theodicy. While a strong argument may be made for faithful sentiments such as found in 19:25–27, the original text is corrupt and notoriously difficult to translate and be more questioning about divine justice than modern translations might suggest.

While the book may have advanced through stages, beginning with a tale about the pious Job, the poetic story seems better suited to events such as the Babylonian exile or the Jewish holocaust, where Job represents the suffering Jewish community. In the end, Job's story is the story of suffering people everywhere; in a prototypical way, Job represents the struggling believer, the person of faith who experiences the incongruities of life without giving up on him/herself or on God.

Recommended Readings (passages separated by semicolons indicate chapters; passages separated by colons indicate verses)

Chapters 1–3; 28–42

Psalms

Introductory Overview

The book of Psalms, a collection of 150 prayers, songs, liturgies, and poems also known as the Psalter, has been the hymnal of the Jews. The spiritual depth and beauty of the psalms make them a treasury of public and private devotion. While the original Hebrew title means "Praises," the poems vary widely in tone and subject. Some express contrition or call down curses, while others are meant to teach. Still others seem to have been written or adapted for use on special occasions, such as coronations or royal weddings. Christians have regarded many as messianic, being quoted in this light by New Testament authors.

Divided into five collections or books, many are ascribed to King David, and are introduced with superscriptions such as "of David." Others are ascribed to temple singers ("Sons of Korah") or "to Asaph," one of David's musicians. Despite such ascriptions, most took their present form during the postexilic period (between 537 and 100 BCE), although some surely are as early as David and even earlier. An important feature of Hebrew poetry, found in the psalms, proverbs, and some prophetic oracles, is parallelism, whereby two or more sections of text are repeated or contrasted, only in different words.

Recommended Readings (passages separated by semicolons indicate chapters; passages separated by colons indicate verses)

Psalms (Book I): 1; 2; 5; 6; 8; 13; 14; 15; 16; 18; 19; 22; 23; 24; 27; 29; 30; 32; 33; 37; 39; 40; 41. (Book II): 42; 43; 45; 46; 49; 51; 55; 61; 62; 63; 65; 67; 69; 72. (Book III): 73; 78; 82; 84; 87; 88; 89. (Book IV): 90; 91; 92; 95; 96; 97; 98; 100; 102; 103; 104. (Book V): 107; 108; 110; 111; 114; 116; 117; 118; 119: 1–20, 105–112, 129–136, 161–176; 121; 122; 123; 127; 128; 130; 131; 133; 139; 144; 145; 148; 150

Proverbs

Introductory Overview

Proverbs is one of three books of wisdom in the Old Testament; the others are Job and Ecclesiastes. Sirach and the Wisdom of Solomon, both deuterocanonical, are wisdom texts and contain recommended readings as well. In its broadest sense, wisdom denotes expertise or skill gained from careful observation of God's created and moral order. Thus, the goal of wisdom is practical success in everyday life, gained primarily through the shaping of character.

As it stands, Proverbs is a compendium of moral and religious instructions given to Jewish youth by professional sages in the postexilic period. The underlying presupposition is that "the fear of the Lord (essentially viewed as an attitude of reverence) is the beginning of wisdom." Proverbs represents different collections of proverbs stemming from various localities and spanning a period from the ninth to the third century BCE. Despite formal attribution to Solomon, Proverbs makes creative use of non-Israelite wisdom traditions from Mesopotamia and Egypt.

After a brief prologue (1:1–7), the first half of the book (1:8–9:18) consists of ten long wisdom speeches interspersed with four interludes that feature wisdom personified as a woman. The second half of the book (10:1–39:9) presents short sayings that describe wise and foolish behavior. The following passages are representative: 10:1–32; 13:1–25; 15:1–23; and 22:1–22. An acrostic poem describing an ideal wife (likely the woman personified as Wisdom in chapters 1–9) comprises the epilogue to the book.

Recommended Readings (passages separated by semicolons indicate chapters; passages separated by colons indicate verses)

Chapters 1–9; 31:10–31

Ecclesiastes

Introductory Overview

Like other biblical wisdom literature, Ecclesiastes has a timeless quality and is concerned with human experience rather than with certainty. Because Ecclesiastes finds little value in certainty or in the principle of just reward and punishment, the author (Qoheleth or "Teacher") expresses profound doubt and questions any principle of fairness. Noting wisdom's limitations and affirming the transience of life, Qoheleth nevertheless portrays God as the creator and sustainer of human life.

Recommended Readings (passages separated by semicolons indicate chapters; passages separated by colons indicate verses)

While this book is a favorite of skeptics and seekers and may be read in its entirety, the miscellaneous observations in chapter 10 may be omitted.

Wisdom of Solomon[1]

Introductory Overview

Though attributed to Solomon, the book of Wisdom was composed in Greek by an unknown Hellenistic Jew around 50 BCE, probably at Alexandria, Egypt, then the largest Jewish center in the Diaspora. The author, denouncing Jewish skeptics of the day who had forsaken inherited beliefs and practices, writes to safeguard the faith of the rest of the people. He does so by offering reward and punishment after death, by portraying Wisdom as a savior of Israel's ancestors, by identifying Wisdom with the spirit of the Lord, and by proposing a religious philosophy of history. Aided by the Greek distinction of body from soul and by Greek ideas of providence, conscience, and the cardinal virtues, the author uses this synthesis to appeal also to pagans to examine Judaism as a valid Wisdom and way of life. The

---

1. This book, one of the apocryphal/deuterocanonical books, appears in ecumenical Bibles as well as in Roman Catholic and Eastern Orthodox Bibles.

book of Wisdom has canonical status in the Eastern Orthodox and Roman Catholic Church while in Protestant denominations it is relegated to the Apocrypha. In the early Christian church, the book was regarded as scripture, and some even included it in the New Testament canon (the book is cited among the list of books held to be canonical in the Muratorian Canon, which appeared about 180 CE).

Recommended Readings (passages separated by semicolons indicate chapters; passages separated by colons indicate verses)

Chapters 1–3; 6:12–25; 7–9

Sirach (Ecclesiasticus)[2]

Introductory Overview

Known as Ecclesiasticus or the Wisdom of Ben Sirach (often Sirach for short), Sirach is one of the few biblical books actually written by the author to whom it is attributed. Written by a sage who identifies himself as "the son of Sirach," the book first appeared in Hebrew around 180 BCE, but it was preserved in Greek by the author's grandson around 117 BCE. Because the Hebrew version fell into disuse, it was not accepted into the Hebrew canon, although its Greek translation, like the Wisdom of Solomon, was included in the Septuagint (the Greek Old Testament), and thus became part of the scriptures in the early Christian community. As a wisdom teacher, Sirach's book resembles the book of Proverbs. Though traditional Jewish wisdom literature rarely appealed to Israel's sacred history or to Israel's covenant, Sirach is an outstanding exception, as his "Praise of the Ancestors" in chapters 44–50 makes clear.

Recommended Readings (passages separated by semicolons indicate chapters; passages separated by colons indicate verses)

Sirach contains three great wisdom poems (chapters 1; 24; 51), which comprise its recommended reading.

---

2. This book, one of the apocryphal/deuterocanonical books, appears in ecumenical Bibles as well as in Roman Catholic and Eastern Orthodox Bibles.

Song of Songs

Introductory Overview

Known as Song of Solomon or the Canticle of Canticles, this book differs from all other books of the Bible in that it consists of love poetry. Interpreted in multiple ways throughout its history, some of these poems originally may have been used in wedding celebrations, a practice that continues in Judaism today. While the book may be divided into some fifteen poems, the book may be read as words spoken by two lovers or as a play. In its present form, a certain flow may be detected, though its unity is one of dialogue rather than of pre-arranged acts. Essentially love poetry, the book was included in the biblical canon as an allegory of God's love for Israel or of Christ's love for the church.

Read literally, these poems serve as a corrective to forms of Judaism and Christianity that consider sexual activity defiling and sexual sins as most threatening to piety and salvation. Nevertheless, because of its graphic and sensual imagery, I suggest deleting the book in favor of biblical passages such as 1 Corinthians 13, Ephesians 5:21–33, and Proverbs 5:5–19 and 31:10–31, where faithfulness to one's spouse is central. In addition, Song of Songs may be eliminated in favor of the apocryphal book of Tobit, with its famous prayer for God's protection and blessing of marriage (Tob 8:4–9).

Recommended Readings (passages separated by semicolons indicate chapters; passages separated by colons indicate verses)

While skipping the book is advised, particularly by children and immature believers, passages such as 2:1–4 and the climax of the love play in 8:6–7 are lovely and highly recommended.

Tobit[3]

Introductory Overview

The book of Tobit is a fictional story of pious and faithful Jews exiled in Assyria. Tobit, whose blindness and poverty are the direct result of burying an executed Jew, recovers his sight and fortune through the courageous efforts of his devoted son Tobias, who is assisted by the angel Raphael disguised

---

3. This book, one of the apocryphal/deuterocanonical books, appears in ecumenical Bibles as well as in Roman Catholic and Eastern Orthodox Bibles.

as a human. Tobias is able to marry Sarah, a blameless young woman who was unable to marry because a demon claimed the lives of her fiancés on their wedding night. With the help of Raphael, Tobias is able to exorcise the demon from Sarah and marry her, reversing the family's fortunes. The entertaining tale emphasizes the importance of piety and family loyalty, making the point that ultimately God protects and rewards the righteous.

Recommended Readings (passages separated by semicolons indicate chapters; passages separated by colons indicate verses)

Like Ruth and Esther, this inspiring tale should be read in its entirety.

Chapter 6

OLD TESTAMENT LITERATURE, PART II

Overview and Passages

THIS CHAPTER, THE SECOND on the books of the Old Testament, provides a brief introduction to the Major Prophets as well as the books of Lamentations, Daniel, and the twelve Minor Prophets, each in literary sequence (namely, in their biblical order). Each introductory overview is followed by a list of recommended readings from that book of the Bible. A complete guide of daily readings, designed to lead individuals through the sixty-six books of the Bible (plus several of the apocryphal/deuterocanonical books) in eleven months or less, is provided in the appendix to this book.

THE PROPHETIC LITERATURE

Isaiah

Introductory Overview

Isaiah is the first of the three Major Prophets, that is, of the three longest prophetic books. Its position as the first reflects the fact that Isaiah lived in the eighth century (prophesying from 742 until 701 or perhaps until 689 BCE), whereas Jeremiah and Ezekiel lived 150 years later. The late eighth century was the critical period in which the Northern Kingdom (Israel) was annexed to the Assyrian empire, while the Southern Kingdom (Judah) lived uneasily in its shadow as a tributary. This is also the period of Hosea and Amos in the North and Micah in the South.

While the book of Isaiah may be considered a unity theologically, it is not so historically. Rather, scholars agree that the book contains oracles from two or perhaps three prophets, designated as First, Second or Deutero-Isaiah, and Third or Trito-Isaiah. Broadly speaking, First Isaiah's literary work consists of Isaiah 1–39, although chapters 24–27 and 34–35 are from a later period. In this section, the author exhibits an exalted view of the Davidic monarchy, believing it to be divinely chosen and eternally favored. Second Isaiah (chapters 40–55) is exilic, dating to about 545–540, to the period immediately before the end of the Babylonian exile. In joyful anticipation of exiled Judah's restoration to its homeland, Second Isaiah emphasizes the significance of historical events in God's sovereign plan.

Chapters 56–66, commonly called Third Isaiah, date to the postexilic period, about 530–510 BCE (the period of Haggai and Zechariah). Third Isaiah's comforting assurance to the restored exiles is tempered by the sobering realities of life in the restored community. Isaiah's unifying message through these three trying segments of history is a vision of assured hope for God's people in a world whose times are in God's hands. During the church age, Isaiah's prophecies of the coming Messiah have frequently been applied to the historical Jesus.

Recommended Readings (passages separated by semicolons indicate chapters; passages separated by colons indicate verses)

Chapters 1:1–2:5; 5–9; 11–12; 25–28; 29:13–24; 30:8–31:9; 32–33; 35; 39–45; 49–56; 58–66

Jeremiah

Introductory Overview

Written against the backdrop of the destruction caused by Babylon's three invasions of Judah from 597–587 and the fall of Jerusalem to the Babylonians in 586, the book of Jeremiah consists of a collection of oracles against Judah and Jerusalem, which he dictated to his aide Baruch. The material is intensely personal—no other prophetic book gives as much biographical information about its namesake—yet biography is not the point. What one learns about Jeremiah's life in this book is always related to the book's double metaphor: plucking up and breaking down of the false and wicked must precede planting and building of the true and righteous. What God calls Jeremiah to proclaim—that God will use Babylon to destroy Jerusalem, and whoever resists Babylon resists God's will—sounds traitorous and evokes much personal suffering and lament.

The material in Jeremiah is not in chronological order and thus is marked by confusions and conflicting emotions. When Jerusalem fell, Jeremiah was not among those taken into exile in Babylon, but later a band of conspirators took him with them to Egypt, where his story ends. One of the high points of Jeremiah's message is the promise that God will make a new covenant with his people, writing his law on their hearts (31:31–34).

Recommended Readings (passages separated by semicolons indicate chapters; passages separated by colons indicate verses)

Chapters 1–4; 7:1–29; 8:18–9:24; 11:1–14:16; 15:5–18:12; 19–34; 36–43; 50:1–51:58; 52:28–34

Lamentations

Introductory Overview

The book of Lamentations is a collection of five communal laments over Jerusalem, following its destruction to the Babylonians in 586, While these psalms have been traditionally assigned to Jeremiah, the thought and diction are sufficiently unlike Jeremiah's to make his authorship unlikely.

Recommended Readings (passages separated by semicolons indicate chapters; passages separated by colons indicate verses)

2:1–22; 2:13–15; 3:1–6, 16–18, 22–23

Ezekiel

Introductory Overview

Deported to Babylon in 597 BCE, eleven years before the fall of Jerusalem, Ezekiel, a priest and the most unique of Israel's prophets, dramatized his prophecies by bizarre actions such as sleeping on one side, not mourning the death of his wife, and eating a scroll. His ministry, beginning in the last years of the kingdom of Judah and ending during the Babylonian captivity (593–571), bridged the greatest catastrophe and transformation the religion of Israel ever experienced: the transition from a religion identified with a land, a monarchy, and a temple to a religion identified with a community of people, thus leading to the essential Judaism of today, which revolves around the synagogue, where the study of the Jewish law is paramount.

After seeing a remarkable vision of God's glory (1:4–28) and commanded to speak only when addressed by God (3:26–27), Ezekiel discovered his overwhelming prophetic task. His prophesy falls into three main divisions: the oracles of warning (chapters 1–24), dated before the fall of Jerusalem; the oracles against foreign nations (chapters 25–32), dated to the middle period of his ministry (587 to 585); and the oracles of hope (chapters 33–48), including the vision of the valley of dry bones (37:1–14) and of the restored temple in Jerusalem (chapters 40–48), dated after the fall of Jerusalem. As a prophet to the exiles, Ezekiel assured his hearers of the abiding presence of God among them. Furthermore, he underscored the integrity of the individual and each person's personal responsibility to God (see chapter 18). In the innovativeness with which he employed the language of vision, Ezekiel (together with Third Isaiah) laid the groundwork for the symbolic universe of apocalypticism, displayed so profoundly in the biblical books of Daniel and Revelation

Recommended Readings (passages separated by semicolons indicate chapters; passages separated by colons indicate verses)

Chapters 1–5; 8–9; 11:14–18:32; 24; 33:21–34:31; 36:22–37:28; 39:1–40:4; 47:1–12, 21–23; 48:30–35

Daniel

Introductory Overview

The six traditional tales and four dream-visions of the book of Daniel make up the only apocalyptic book in the Old Testament. The first half of Daniel (chapters 1–6), a cycle of court legends about Daniel and his three companions, focuses on religious loyalty and the challenges arising when Jews live in a hostile, foreign environment. The second half (chapter 7–12) narrates David's apocalyptic visions regarding the fate of Israel in the end time, believed to be imminent. While the stories of Daniel and his friends are set in the exilic period in Babylon just before and after the Persian conquest (mid to late sixth century BCE), chapters 7–12 were composed during the Maccabean revolt, reaching their present form around 164 BCE, thus making Daniel the most recent (youngest) book in the Hebrew Bible.[1] Early Christians found in the Son of Man figure in Daniel 7:13–14 a prophecy about Jesus.

Recommended Readings (passages separated by semicolons indicate chapters; passages separated by colons indicate verses)

Chapters 1–7; 12:1–4

THE MINOR PROPHETS

Hosea

Introductory Overview

Hosea is the first of the twelve Minor Prophets. The title of "minor" is not a measure of significance but of length. By the second century BCE, these twelve short scrolls constituted the Book of the Twelve and because they fit into one scroll, were treated as a literary unit. While Hosea is listed first among these shorter prophets, he is predated by the prophecy of Amos. Like Amos, Hosea prophesied in the northern kingdom of Israel before its destruction in 721 BCE. In this book, Hosea tells of his tragic marriage to Gomer and speaks of his experiences with his unfaithful wife as a parable of God's enduring love for the wayward nation of Israel.

Concerned about idolatry and religious compromise among the people, Hosea develops the theme of Israel's apostasy and unfaithfulness, for which divine judgment rests upon the nation. The first biblical writer to describe the relation between God and Israel in terms of marriage, Hosea's symbolism is carried on in the New Testament with the imagery of the church as the bride of Christ. The book is divided into two uneven parts (chapters 1–3 and 4–16), but is unified by the theme of divine compassion and redeeming love. The book closes with the promise that eventually Israel will be restored.

Recommended Readings (passages separated by semicolons indicate chapters; passages separated by colons indicate verses)

Chapters 1:1–6:6; 9:1–10:6; 11; 14

---

1. Readers interested in this period may want to consult 1 Maccabees, a deuterocanonical (apocryphal) book that covers events of the second century (175–132 BCE).

Old Testament Literature, Part II

Joel

Introductory Overview

Joel uses the devastation of a plague of locusts as God's judgment on the people and calls them to repent. Using this catastrophe as a dire warning, Joel uses it to predict the Day of the Lord (the final judgment). His urgent call to repentance, expressed in apocalyptic language, is followed by a vision of the future, in which God will compensate the people for their suffering as well as punish their enemies. Though little is known of Joel's ministry, textual evidence points to a time after the Babylonian exile, about 400 to 350 BCE. Joel's prophecy predicting the outpouring of God's Spirit on all flesh (2:28–32) is cited in the book of Acts as foreshadowing the gift of the Holy Spirit on Pentecost.

Recommended Readings (passages separated by semicolons indicate chapters; passages separated by colons indicate verses)

Chapters 1:1–3:3; 3:13–21

Amos

Introductory Overview

Considered the first writing prophet, Amos is renowned for championing social justice. In his "I Have a Dream" speech in 1963, Martin Luther King, Jr. appealed to Amos's powerful words as recorded in 5:24. Amos, called by God from his job as a shepherd in the Judean village of Tekoa, went north to the kingdom of Israel sometime during the decade 760–750 BCE to denounce Israel and neighboring countries for grave social injustice, immoral behavior, and reliance on military might. The military security and economic affluence of the long and peaceful reign of Jeroboam II (786–746) were taken by many Israelites as signs of God's special favor. Amos's forceful, uncompromising preaching brought him into conflict with the religious and political authorities of his day. Expelled from the royal sanctuary at Bethel, Amos likely returned to Judah to record his oracles. The book is divided into three parts: oracles against Israel's neighbors (chapters 1–2), indictment of Israel for sin and injustice (chapters 3–6), and visions of Israel's coming doom (chapters 7–9). The book ends on a happier note, promising a glorious age to come (9:11–12).

Recommended Readings (passages separated by semicolons indicate chapters; passages separated by colons indicate verses)

Chapters 1:1–2; 3:1–8; 5:1–24; 7:10–9:6

Obadiah

Introductory Overview

The shortest book of the Old Testament (21 verses), the book of Obadiah was written soon after Jerusalem fell to the Babylonians in 586 BCE. The book contains a prophecy against Edom for hostile actions against the people of Israel. In the biblical tradition, the Edomites were descendants of Esau, Jacob's twin brother, and Edom is indicted for hostile actions against Jacob's descendants. Like Joel, Obadiah announces the Day of the Lord as a day of judgment and as a prediction that Israel's and Edom's national situations will be reversed.

Recommended Readings (passages separated by semicolons indicate chapters; passages separated by colons indicate verses)

Due to vengeful and its imprecatory nature, this book may be skipped in its entirety.

Jonah

Introductory Overview

Unlike other prophetic books of the Old Testament, Jonah contains no collection of oracles against Israel and foreign nations. Instead, it presents the story of Jonah, called to preach against the wickedness of Nineveh and the Assyrians. Unlike other prophets, Jonah disobeys God's call and heads in the opposite direction to which he is commanded to go. During a storm at sea, he is cast overboard, and is swallowed by a fish. After surviving in the fish's belly for three days and nights, he goes to Nineveh, whose entire population repents. Because a literal account of the prophet's adventures cannot be sustained, the book is interpreted allegorically, satirically, or as a parable. Although the prophet lived in the time of Jeroboam II (see 2 Kgs 14:25), the book seems to have been written at least two to four centuries later, after the destruction of Nineveh in 612 BCE. On account of its universalism and its opposition to the narrow sectarianism and exclusiveness found in Ezra and Nehemiah, the book likely originated in the later fifth or early fourth centuries (after 400 BCE).

Recommended Readings (passages separated by semicolons indicate chapters; passages separated by colons indicate verses)

Valuable for its moral and theological teaching, this interesting tale should be read in its entirety.

Micah

Introductory Overview

A Judean prophet, Micah was a younger contemporary of Isaiah (eight century BCE). Unlike Isaiah, Micah was neither of noble descent nor a native of Jerusalem. Rather, he came from a small rural village in the Judean foothills southwest of Jerusalem, close to the Philistine city of Gath. Micah witnessed and preached about the fall of Israel (at that time called "Samaria"), when it officially was annexed to Assyria. The author was painfully aware of the devastation caused by the Assyrians as they continued their conquests southward into Philistia and the southern foothills of Judah.

The oracles preserved in Micah are addressed mainly to the inhabitants of Jerusalem. Micah's rural upbringing may have given him extra sensitivity for the suffering of the poor and powerless, whom he championed in his preaching. While the final words of the book offer a tone of compassion, Micah makes it clear that God will not tolerate injustice, hypocrisy, and disregard for the covenant relationship. The book is a collection of short oracles written in a variety of styles. Some of the prophecies, such as the picture of the restored Jerusalem in 7:8-28, come from a later hand and are dated to the postexilic period. Noteworthy in the latter chapters is Micah's intercession on behalf of the people (6:6–8), culminating in one of the most often quoted passages of the entire Bible (6:8), as well as Micah's prediction of the coming of a messianic ruler who is to be born in Bethlehem, a passage quoted by Matthew in connection with the birth of Jesus (Matt 2:6; see also John 7:42).

Recommended Readings (passages separated by semicolons indicate chapters; passages separated by colons indicate verses)

Chapters 1:1; 4:11–5:4; 6:1–8; 7:14–20

Nahum

Introductory Overview

Prompted by the dramatic events leading up to the fall of the hated Assyrian empire, Nahum utters a devastating oracle against Assyria and its capital Nineveh. For centuries, Assyria had been like a lion preying on and dominating other nations of the eastern Mediterranean region (known by scholars as the ancient Near East). Israel had fallen to Assyria in 721, and Judah had become a vassal of Assyria at that time and remained so for most of the seventh century. With the destruction of Nineveh by a coalition of Babylonians and Medes in 612 BCE, Assyrian domination came to an end.

The core of Nahum's prophecy is a vivid poem extolling Nineveh's destruction. Though the book belongs in the category of "oracle against the nations," the description of Nineveh's fall is so vivid that the book must have been written shortly thereafter. Thus, the book comes after Micah (the last eighth century Judean prophet) and Habakkuk (who anticipates the rise of Babylon). While the book is an obvious celebration of vengeance, Micah's deeper message forces Judah to reconsider its own fate should its social and religious failures continue. However, the book's concluding message is also consoling: if we trust God, no enemy can destroy us.

Recommended Readings (passages separated by semicolons indicate chapters; passages separated by colons indicate verses)

Despite its closing message, the book is primarily a prophecy against ancient Nineveh and may be skipped in its entirety.

Habakkuk

Introductory Overview

Dated to the late seventh century and to the latter years of Jeremiah's prophetic career, the first two chapters of Habakkuk function as a complaint against the prosperity of Judah's wealthy and warn the populace of Judah of God's promise to send the Babylonians to punish them. Following the defeat of Egypt at Carchemish in 605 BCE, the Babylonians took control of Judah. This led to a Judean revolt against Babylon in 598 and to the first deportation of many prominent Judeans to Babylon in 597. The book of Habakkuk addresses the question of unjust suffering and evil. Chapters 1 and

2 present the prophet's dialogue with the Lord, and God's response comes in 2:2–20, with a statement that the wicked will fall and the righteous will live by their faithfulness (2:4). Because of its use by Paul in Romans 1:17 and Galatians 3:11 (see also Heb 10:38–39), Habakkuk's reference to "faithfulness" (or "faith") became important in Christian thought as the starting point of the necessity of faith for salvation. Habakkuk's closing chapter (3:3–15) is a liturgical psalm in which God answers the prophet with a theophanic description of his divine defeat of the wicked.

Recommended Readings (passages separated by semicolons indicate chapters; passages separated by colons indicate verses)

The prophecy of Habakkuk should be read in its entirety.

Zephaniah

Introductory Overview

Dated to the rule of Josiah, righteous king of Judah (640–609 BCE), Zephaniah announces the coming Day of the Lord, pronouncing judgment on Judah for its religious syncretism (1:2–2:3) and against the nations (2:4–15). Zephaniah concludes with a series of promises for all who repent and turn to God. In many respects, Zephaniah functions as the southern counterpart of Amos in the north, pronouncing judgment against Judah and the nations. However, unlike Amos, Zephaniah depicts God and not a Davidic monarch as king of the restored Zion (3:15; see also Amos 9:11, cited as a fulfilled prophecy in Acts 15:16). Central to Zephaniah's theology is his understanding of sin as an offence against the majesty of the living God.

Recommended Readings (passages separated by semicolons indicate chapters; passages separated by colons indicate verses)

Chapters 1:1–3; 3:1–20

Haggai

Introductory Overview

When the Persian ruler Cyrus conquered Babylon in 539 BCE, he issued a decree allowing a return of Judean exiles, but their effort to raise a new temple faltered after the erection of an altar and repair of the temple's foundation. The exhortation of Haggai, together with Zechariah, resulted in the new temple's dedication in 515. The purpose of Haggai's inspiring preaching was to awaken popular resolve for the completion of the second temple, the first having been destroyed by the Babylonians in 586. In five addresses, dated to the year 520, Haggai exhorted Zerubbabel the governor and Joshua the high priest, the joint leaders of the Judean community, to reconstruct the temple, and urged the priests to purify the cultic worship. As Haggai saw it, these two steps would both unify the community and prepare for the messianic age, that wonderful era foreseen by earlier prophets. At this time God would bless the Jewish people with prosperity and restore David's dynasty, with Zerubbabel as messianic king (2:20–23).

Recommended Readings (passages separated by semicolons indicate chapters; passages separated by colons indicate verses)

Chapters 1:1–2:9; 2:20–23

Zechariah

Introductory Overview

A priest in the early restoration era (520–518), Zechariah shared the zeal of Haggai to rebuild the temple in preparation for God's tangible presence. As a Zadokite priest, he eventually was placed in charge of an entire priestly clan. The book of Zechariah consists of at least two distinct works. The first eight chapters, known as First Zechariah, may have circulated for a while as a composite work with the book of Haggai. The next six chapters (9–14), a collection of separated apocalyptic prophecies, was attached by Zechariah's disciples at a later time. Whereas First Zechariah reflects the early Persian period, the prophecies of Deutero-Zechariah differ in style, vocabulary, and theological ideas and were written during the Greek period, principally in the fourth and third centuries BCE. Some of these prophecies are thought to be later yet, perhaps following the Maccabean War, which ended about 160 BCE. While much of chapters 9–14 is enigmatic, the battle scene in 14:1–5 has an apocalyptic cast.

First Zechariah's peaceful images of the messianic king (4:1–4, 11–14; 6:9–15) replace Haggai's more violent imagery of royal restoration (Hag 2:20–23). Deutero-Zechariah's description of the triumphant coming of the humble king (9:9) was taken by New Testament writers as prefiguring Jesus' entry into Jerusalem on Palm Sunday (see Matt 21:2–7; John 12:14–15).

First Zechariah states his message partly in oracles (see chapters 7–8), but mostly in visions of God's purification of Jerusalem (chapters 1–6). These highly symbolic visions foreshadow the style that apocalyptic books such as Daniel and Revelation would later develop.

Recommended Readings (passages separated by semicolons indicate chapters; passages separated by colons indicate verses)

Chapters 1–6; 9:9–10:12; 12:10–14:21

Malachi

Introductory Overview

Little is known about the person of Malachi; even his name, which means "my messenger" (3:1), may be only a title. Through internal evidence, the book is dated to the early Persian period (500-450 BCE); the prophet was devoted to the temple and esteemed the priesthood. Like Ezra and Nehemiah, he opposed mixed marriage and exhorted faithfulness to the Lord's covenant and its teaching. The answer to the people's constant question, "Where is the God of justice?" (2:17) is given in 3:1 by the coming of a promised "messenger of the covenant," who will serve as herald. In the New Testament this prophecy is taken by the gospel writers as fulfilled in John the Baptist (Mark 1:2; see also Matt 3:3 and Isa 40:3). The messenger who "prepares the way" and the sending of Elijah (Mal 4:5) suggested to the gospel writers a connection with the coming of the Messiah (Matt 11:7–15; Mark 9:11–13; Luke 1:16–17). Malachi 4:4–6 draws Malachi and the Bible's entire collection of prophecy to a close. Deuteronomy 34:10–12 concludes the Torah on a similar note. The revelation to Moses was foundational, but in addition to mediating the Lord's covenant, Moses was also a prophet, and he had prophets as successors (see Deut 18:15–19).

Recommended Readings (passages separated by semicolons indicate chapters; passages separated by colons indicate verses)

Chapters 1; 3–4

Chapter 7

NEW TESTAMENT LITERATURE, PART I
Overview and Passages

THIS CHAPTER, THE FIRST of two chapters on the books of the New Testament, provides a brief introduction to the gospels, the book of Acts, and the first nine biblical letters attributed to Paul, all in literary sequence (namely, in their biblical order). Each introductory overview is followed by a list of recommended readings from that book of the Bible. A complete guide of daily readings, designed to lead individuals through the sixty-six books of the Bible (plus several of the apocryphal/deuterocanonical books) in eleven months or less, is provided in the appendix to this book.

THE GOSPELS

The four gospels provide overlapping yet unique accounts of the life and teaching of Jesus of Nazareth, whom they call Jesus the Christ. The first three gospels follow a similar pattern, based on the prototype given by Mark, whereas the fourth gospel (John) diverges in significant ways. The approach I recommend is to begin with Mark, and then to add important divergent readings from Matthew and Luke. Our study of the gospels ends with John's gospel. While some redundancy or parallel passages in the recommended readings are retained to maintain continuity, particularly in passages dealing with the crucifixion and resurrection of Jesus, in all cases the flow of the story is provided in Mark's account, whose sequence readers are encouraged to follow.

New Testament Literature, Part I

Like the other New Testament books and most of the rest of the Bible, the gospels are the literary productions of a believing community. Since the gospels are written in narrative form, it is easy to assume that they are an accurate record of the life and teachings of Jesus. While they contain reliable information, they are not primarily biographical but rather inspirational and exhortatory in nature, as Luke 1:4 and John 20:31 make clear. In addition, each gospel writer is both an author and a theologian, writing from a unique perspective to a different audience and presenting a distinct portrait of Jesus.

Mark

Introductory Overview

Writing in a distinct literary and theological style, Mark presents Jesus as a Servant of God, by which title he describes an individual close to God and totally dedicated to God's purpose and will for humanity. Because Mark is regarded as the first of the four gospels (written about 70 CE, some forty years after the crucifixion of Jesus), we start with this account of his life and teaching. Mark's ordering of the life and ministry of Jesus greatly influenced the gospels of Matthew and Luke, which never agree together in sequence against Mark. For that reason, the first three gospels are called the Synoptic Gospels, unlike John's gospel, which, written last, takes a distinctly different approach.

Unlike the other gospels, Mark's gospel contains few parables or discourses of Jesus, and unlike Matthew and Luke, Mark opens not with the birth of Jesus but with the ministry of John the Baptist, who is presented as the fulfillment of prophecy, and then moves quickly through the baptism and temptation of Jesus to his ministry. Mark's gospel can be divided into four parts: the Galilean ministry (chapters 1–9); the journey to Jerusalem (chapter 10); the passion material, focusing on the last week in the life of Jesus (chapter 11–15); and ending with an incomplete account of the resurrection (16:1–8). Because the gospel seems to end abruptly, it contains a shorter and longer ending, added later by unknown writers. Due to their focus on the trial, crucifixion, and burial of Jesus, the gospels have been called passion accounts with long introductions. Although the first gospel is anonymous, tradition ascribes it to John Mark (see Acts 12:12; 15:37), who is said to have composed his gospel at Rome as a summary of Peter's preaching (see 1 Pet 5:13).

Recommended Readings (passages separated by semicolons indicate chapters; passages separated by colons indicate verses)

On account of the gospel's priority, and because it serves as a template for Matthew and Luke's account, Mark's gospel should be read in its entirety, ending with the secondary ending (16:9–20).

Matthew

Introductory Overview

Written some ten to fifteen years after Mark, Matthew writes from a distinctly Jewish Christian perspective, describing Jesus as Israel's royal Messiah, accentuating his descent from King David and the royal line of kings of Judah. Traditionally placed first in the New Testament canon, Matthew describes Jesus as the fulfiller and the fulfillment of God's will as disclosed in the Old Testament. A noteworthy feature of this gospel is its collection of Jesus teachings into five discourses, beginning with the Sermon on the Mount (chapters 5–7) and continuing with discourses in chapters 10, 12, 18, and finally with the discourse on eschatology in chapters 25–25. Some scholars consider the fivefold discourses as patterned after the Pentateuch (the five books of Torah), appropriate to an audience familiar with the Old Testament, to whom Jesus is presented as the new or second Moses (see Deut 18:15, 18).

Unlike Mark, Matthew's gospel begins with the birth of Jesus (chapters 1–2) and has a more complete account of the resurrection, ending with a resurrection appearance to his disciples and an apostolic commission in 28:18–20. As the only gospel writer to use the word "church" (see 6:18 and 18:17), the gospel of Matthew may be seen as a manual of Christian teaching in which Jesus is Lord of God's ongoing new-yet-old community of the faithful (a uniquely Matthean version of discipline in this ecclesiastical community appears in 18:15–20, as well as the famous teaching of Jesus regarding radical discipleship in the parable of the great judgment in 25:31–46).

Recommended Readings (passages separated by semicolons indicate chapters; passages separated by colons indicate verses)

Chapters 1:18-2:23; 5–7; 12:38–45; 18:1–19:2; 20:1–19; 21:1–32; 23:1–39; 25:1–13; 25:31–26:16; 27:15–28:20

New Testament Literature, Part I

Luke

Introductory Overview

Written shortly after Matthew, the author, a Greek convert to Judaism, envisages a Gentile rather than a Jewish audience. Thus, he makes few quotations from the Old Testament, which would have been almost unknown to most non-Jews. Luke, as a highly skilled and educated author, writes in a sublime literary style, and his gospel has been called "the most beautiful book in the world." During advent season, it is his version of the birth narrative that is most often read in church, since it is the most familiar and beloved. In his gospel, Luke emphasizes the humanity of Jesus and the concern of Jesus with all humanity, particularly the poor and disadvantages, and includes numerous references that concerned Samaritans, then viewed as members of a despised race.

Luke, said to have been a physician and a traveling companion of the apostle Paul, also emphasizes Jesus' concern for women, even telling the story of the birth of Jesus from Mary's point of view. Another noteworthy point is Luke's insistence that the teaching of Jesus and promise of salvation is addressed to all people, not simply to the Jews or to enlightened Gentiles. In the gospel's middle section, known as Luke's Travel Narrative (9;51–19:48), Luke includes more episodes of Jesus' final journey to Jerusalem than any of the other gospels. Luke's gospel does not end with the resurrection and ascension of Jesus but continues in a sequel book of Acts. Like Acts, Luke's gospel also assigns a prominent place to both prayer and the action of the Holy Spirit.

Recommended Readings (passages separated by semicolons indicate chapters; passages separated by colons indicate verses)

Chapters 1:1–3:22; 4:1–30; 7:1–35; 9:51–10:42; 11:37–12:21; 13:1–17; 13:31–18:14; 19:1–48; 21:5–36; 22:54–24:53

John

Introductory Overview

Significantly differing from the Synoptic Gospels, John's gospel is unique in arrangement and sequence as well as in its view of Jesus, depicted as the eternal Son of God. Lacking a genealogy or a birth narrative, the gospel begins with a magnificent prologue (1:1–18), which sets forth Jesus Christ as the divine Logos or Word of God. Incarnate in human flesh, Jesus makes known the will and ways of the invisible God (1:18). Written for all believers, John presents a spiritual Jesus and uses a symbolic approach to Jesus' profound teaching. Although the gospel only contains seven miracles of Jesus (called "signs"), most appear only in this gospel. John's gospel is also distinct in that it records no parables of Jesus. Rather, the gospel presents seven discourses or similitudes, known as "I Am Sayings," in which Jesus uses symbolically common terms such as bread, water, light, life, word, shepherd, door, and way to describe himself and the nature of his ministry. This gospel also features Jesus' conflict with unbelievers (chapters 5–12); his fellowship with believers (chapters 13–17); greatly enlarges the Synoptic version of the trial, death, and resurrection of Jesus (chapters 18–20); and concludes with a unique epilogue (chapter 21). Although tradition ascribes the fourth gospel to the apostle John, who in this gospel speaks as an unnamed "beloved disciple" (21:7, 20; see also 19:35 and 21:24), most scholars consider the author to have been a disciple of John, who recorded John's preaching as Mark did that of Peter. The gospel of John, written some five to ten years after Luke, was produced near the close of the first century, about 95 CE.

Recommended Readings (passages separated by semicolons indicate chapters; passages separated by colons indicate verses)

Due to its uniqueness and its value as the most prized gospel by believers of all ages, this gospel, like Mark, is to be read in its entirety.

The Gospel of Thomas

Introductory Overview

Though not a book in the canonical New Testament, the Gospel of Thomas is recommended reading for those interested in the context and background of the canonical gospels. Containing a collection of 114 sayings attributed to Jesus, this gospel is dated to the first century by a few biblical scholars, although most scholars consider it much better dated to the mid or late second century. While many of the saying in Thomas are familiar to those who have read the gospels of the New Testament, some are quite unlike anything known from the New Testament.

Known as the Coptic Gospel of Thomas (to distinguish it from the Infancy Gospel of Thomas), the Coptic Gospel was accidentally uncovered by a farmer near the village of Nag Hammadi, Egypt, in 1945, about a year before the discovery of Cave 1 of the Dead Sea Scrolls. Unlike much of the gnostic literature, the Gospel of Thomas is a beautiful expression of nondual wisdom. In this text, Jesus appears as a person seeking to awaken his readers to their own state of consciousness.

Recommended Readings (the Gospel of Thomas is worth reading in its entirety).

The Community Rule

Introductory Overview

This volume, also known as the Manual of Discipline, is part of the Dead Sea Scrolls, most of which were written shortly before the time of Jesus by a sect with some similar beliefs and practices to the followers of John the Baptist and to the first followers of Jesus. Between 1947 and 1956, eleven caves discovered near Qumran on the western shore of the Dead Sea, yielded many scrolls and fragments of scrolls known collectively as the Dead Sea Scrolls. The community of Qumran, likely a strict Essene Jewish sect, devoutly and avidly studied the Hebrew scriptures (copies or fragments of every book of the Bible save Esther have been found at Qumran), including apocryphal books in the Septuagint such as Tobit and Sirach, in addition to pseudepigraphic books popular in certain Jewish circles of the time. The sectarian Dead Sea Scrolls, thought to have been composed or revised by the Qumran community, comprise rule books, Bible commentaries, apocalypses, and other religious and esoteric writings.

Of these, one of the most important documents is the Community Rule, originally composed around 100 BCE. This work, likely intended for the community's teachers (its Masters or Overseers), contains extracts from liturgical ceremonies and statutes concerned with initiation into the sect and its common life. In addition, the manual includes an introduction to the sect's core teaching regarding the spirits of truth and falsehood that are said to separate the children (sons) of light from the children (sons) of darkness. Unique to the Scrolls is a "good versus evil" or "us versus them" kind of thinking that scholars call "dualism." Many of the dualistic expressions found in the Scrolls and also in New Testament writings such as the gospel of John were adopted by early Christian and gnostic thinkers, but such apocalyptic thought is almost absent from other ancient secular and religious literature.

Recommended Readings (passages separated by semicolons indicate chapters; passages separated by colons indicate verses)

Because of the prominence of radical dualist thinking in some sectarian Jewish and Christian groups of the first century, such as the Essenes, the followers of John the Baptist, and the gospel of John, readers of the Bible are encouraged to familiarize themselves with the teaching regarding the spirits of truth and falsehood in Community Rule 3:13–4:26.

Acts

Introductory Overview

A sequel to Luke's gospel, the book of Acts traces the story of the Christian movement from the resurrection of Jesus to the time when the apostle Paul is exiled to Rome awaiting trial while proclaiming the gospel without hindrance (28:31). Thus, Acts takes its place sequentially between the gospels and the letters in the Christian New Testament much like the historical books serve as a transition between the Torah and the Writings in the Jewish Bible. Narrating the progress of the Christian gospel through six chronological phases, Acts describes the ethnic shift in the church's composition from a primarily Jewish core at the beginning to a primarily Gentile composition at the end. Likewise, the author describes the church's geographical shift or movement from Jerusalem to Rome (viewed both as the capital of the Roman empire as well as the center of the envisioned "ends of the earth" in Acts 1:8.

Almost one-fifth of the book consists of speeches and missionary discourses, six to Jewish audiences and two to Gentiles. While the anonymous author's purpose in Acts is to show how the church emerged as a chiefly Gentile universal phenomenon from its origins as a Jerusalem-based group of Jewish believers, he argues that it is the Holy Spirit that is ultimately responsible for this (see 13:2; 16:6–8). In fact, the book, entitled "The Acts of the Apostles," might better be entitled "The Acts of the Holy Spirit," for the dominant theme is the person of the Spirit manifested in and through the members of the early church.

NEW TESTAMENT LITERATURE, PART I

In the first half (chapters 1–12), Peter, the apostle to the Jews, is the hero, whereas in the second half, the hero is Paul, the apostle to the Gentiles. Central to the plot are Peter's speech on the Day of Pentecost (chapter 2) and Stephen's speech to his accusers in chapter 7. Transitional to the missionary journeys and trials of Paul in the second half of the book are the conversions of Paul (Saul) told in chapter 9 and of a Roman centurion named Cornelius, told in chapter 10. Central also to the development of the early Christian movement is the Apostolic Council in Jerusalem (described in chapter 15), where the delegates conclude that Gentiles need not convert to Judaism to become Christian. Since nothing is said about Paul's fate in Rome at the close of the account, the book is popularly dated to about 68 CE, although most scholars disagree, dating it as late as 85 CE, shortly after the publication of Luke's gospel.

Recommended Readings (passages separated by semicolons indicate chapters; passages separated by colons indicate verses)

Chapters 1:1–7:2a; 7:48–25:12; 27–28

PAUL'S LETTERS

Introductory Overview

Unlike the Old Testament, which contains no letters, 21 of the 27 books of the New Testament are letters. Like the other letters in the Old Testament, Paul's letters are arranged in order of length (Romans being the longest and Philemon the shortest). Of the thirteen letters attributed to the apostle Paul, the first 9 are written to churches and the last 4 to individuals. Of his letters, 7 are undisputed in authorship (Romans, 1 and 2 Corinthians, Galatians, Philippians, 1 Thessalonians, and Philemon), and the rest are often attributed to followers of Paul, based on factors such as style, wording, theology, ecclesiology, and historical background. One explanation for differences and incongruities is that Paul often dictated his letters (see Rom 16:22), and the possibility that a close follower of Paul edited fragments of his letters and applied them to later situations (see particularly 1 and 2 Timothy and Titus, known collectively as the Pastoral Epistles.

As with all letters, it is important to remember that they represent one-way conversations, that is, only half of a conversation. Hence, it is important for modern readers to know that these letters were written to address first-century problems and concerns, and as with parables, sometimes details are irrelevant, unimportant, or easily capable of misinterpretation. On the whole, Paul's letters follow a discernable pattern. In addition to introductory and concluding remarks, the middle section of the majority of his letters is divided into two sections: a doctrinal segment followed by a practical segment.

Romans

Introductory Overview

Romans was written at the height of Paul's career, likely from Corinth during his third missionary journey (57–58 CE), on the eve of his sailing back to Jerusalem. His intention was to take a trip to Rome and from there to go as far west as Spain (see Rom 15:24, 28, 32). Unlike most of his other letters, Romans appears not to have been written in response to local problems or to correct doctrinal or moral errors. Until recently, Romans was viewed as a calm, almost systematic exposition of the message Paul was preaching. In recent decades, however, scholars agree that this letter addresses some particular situation at Rome, though there is little agreement on the specifics of the situation. The details likely lie hidden in chapters 9–11, as well as in the practical section that follows.

For Paul, the gospel is God's power for salvation to all who believe (see Rom 1:16–17). His theme is expressed in terms of God's saving righteousness and summarized as justification by faith. The doctrinal section of Rome expresses this theme in three stages: (1) the universal need of righteousness (1:18–3:20); (2) the way to righteousness (3:21–4:24); and (3) the results of righteousness (chapters 5–8). This initial segment is followed by a section discussing God's plan and role for the Jews, viewed as repentant and unrepentant Israel, ending with the controversial statement, "all Israel will be saved" (11:26). The practical section discusses three topics: life in the church (chapter 12); life in the state (chapter 13); and life in relation to "gray" or questionable areas (14:1–15:13).

Recommended Readings (passages separated by semicolons indicate chapters; passages separated by colons indicate verses)

Chapters 1–14

New Testament Literature, Part I

1 Corinthians

Introductory Overview

Because Paul's letters are organized by length, they are best understood chronologically, beginning with 1 Thessalonians. First Corinthians, likely written around 54 CE, was one of several letters written to the church at Corinth, an important city in the Roman province of Achaia (modern-day Greece). It was not, however, the first letter in the extensive Corinthian correspondence; for a previous letter, now lost, see 1 Corinthians 5:9 (some scholars consider 2 Cor 6:14–7:1 a surviving fragment).

The atmosphere at Corinth, a port city notorious for immorality, deeply influenced the Christians in the local church, most of them from the lower classes (Paul calls them "infants in Christ"; see 1 Cor 3:1–3). The church is torn by strife, and its members are deeply divided. To them, Paul addresses three disciplinary lapses evident at Corinth: congregational factions (chapters 1–4), a case of immorality (chapter 5), and lawsuits among Christians (chapter 6). To these believers Paul writes a strong, helpful, and practical letter, responding to at least five different questions they have raised (7:1): (1) concerning marriage and divorce (7:1–24); concerning celibacy (7:25–40); concerning food laws and food offered to idols (8:1–11:1); (4) concerning spiritual gifts (12:1–14:40); and (5) concerning an offering collected by Paul on behalf of impoverished believers in Jerusalem (16:1–12). In settling local doctrinal and ethical problems that were threatening the Corinthian church, Paul included some of the most exalted chapters in his letters, including the hymn on Christian love (chapter 13) and teaching on the meaning of the resurrection (chapter 15).

Recommended Readings (passages separated by semicolons indicate chapters; passages separated by colons indicate verses)

Chapters 1–3; 9; 12:1–14:5; 15

2 Corinthians

Introductory Overview

When Paul wrote 1 Corinthians, he had known the believers there for more than three years. After writing his original (lost) letter, dealing with divisions and immorality, the latter problem was not resolved. Apparently, 1

Corinthians also failed to resolve the disputes. Several more letters and even emergency trips to Corinth followed. What we call 2 Corinthians mentions another lost letter (2:3; 7:8–12) and perhaps contains fragments of at least two more letters. Written about a year after 1 Corinthians, in 2 Corinthians the honeymoon between Paul and the Corinthian church is clearly over. Consequently, much of 2 Corinthians deals with a crisis in confidence between Paul and his church, some of it likely due to rival teachers and opponents (see 4:4–6, 22–23). Criticizing his apostleship, they may also have criticized his collection for the poor in Jerusalem, an issue he addresses in chapters 8–9, as he had done in 1 Corinthians 16.

Having made a "painful visit" to the church at Corinth (2:1), the apostle delayed making another visit. Instead, he had written a severe letter (see 2:3–4; 7:8), likely now 2 Corinthians 10–13 or possibly lost. Meeting his co-worker Titus in Macedonia (2:12–13), who brought a reassuring report on the converted attitude of the Corinthian church toward him (7:5–16; also 2:14–17), Paul responds in gratitude, writing 2 Corinthians (or at least much of chapters 1–9). In this letter, we see Paul's back against the wall, and his response through themes of consolation, reconciliation, and a theology of weakness (see 12:7–10).

Recommended Readings (passages separated by semicolons indicate chapters; passages separated by colons indicate verses)

Chapters 1–5; 10:1–12:10

Galatians

Introductory Overview

Written before Romans and containing Paul's earliest teaching on justification by faith, the letter to the Galatians is one of the most significant of the New Testament. Following a clear argument, the letter displays a threefold pattern: an autobiographical section (chapters 1-2), a doctrinal section (chapters 3–4), and a concluding ethical or practical section (chapters 5–6).

Written about 55 CE, during Paul's third missionary journey, Galatians has been called the Magna Charta of Christian Liberty, for it deals with a question much debated at the earlier Apostolic Council at Jerusalem (see Acts 15), namely, whether Gentiles must become Jews before they can become Christians. Walking midway between legalism and libertinism, two moral extremes in the early church, Paul argues for the priority and necessity of faith (chapters 3–4). Paul's argument is that while keeping the Mosaic Torah or Jewish legal codes cannot guarantee salvation, it does have a remedial function, bringing people to Christ. The key, however, is "faith working through love" (5:6), for love is of God (5:22), and God's love fulfills the whole law (5:13–14). Vying with Judaizing teachers and even with Christian opponents sent by Christian leaders such as James and Peter (Cephas; see 2:11–14), Paul had a hard time explaining the freedom Christ brings to a Jewish or Jewish-Christian public. Galatians represents his best attempt. To support his understanding of the true function of the Mosaic law and its relation to God's grace, manifested in Christ, Paul declares principles that resulted in making Christianity a universal religion instead of a Jewish sect.

Recommended Readings (passages separated by semicolons indicate chapters; passages separated by colons indicate verses)

The letter to the Galatians should be read in its entirety.

Ephesians

Introductory Overview

Written for the church in the city of Ephesus, the Roman capital of Asia Minor and an early center of Christianity, the letter to the Ephesians presents a variety of problems regarding authenticity (authorship) and destination. Paul had spent three years preaching in Ephesus, and yet the letter is strangely impersonal, lacking greetings and containing a number of words and phrases that appear un-Pauline (see also the strange remark in 3:2). To account for these difficulties, scholars have suggested that Ephesians, like Colossians and 2 Thessalonians, may have been written by a later admirer of Paul. Another explanation that addresses specific literary and biographic problems is that Paul's disputed letters were dictated by Paul to different scribes, who took liberties in writing them. Pseudonymous authorship, namely, writing under a false name or to honor a great author or teacher, was common in the biblical world and not considered plagiarism. In the case of Ephesians, a disciple of Paul may have written this letter about 85 or 90 CE in Paul's name to reflect his thought and to apply it to new situations. A common explanation for the impersonal nature of Ephesians is that instead of being intended only for the church at Ephesus, the letter may have been a "circular" letter, that is, sent to a group of churches, of which

Ephesus became the final destination. Such a solution also helps explain why Ephesians reads more like a sermon meditation than a letter. Regardless of who wrote Ephesians, the letter is thoroughly Pauline.

The theme of Ephesians is the church, particularly God's eternal purpose in establishing and completing the universal church of Jesus Christ, thereby uniting Jew and Gentile in "one new humanity in place of the two" (2:15). For this reason, the author emphasizes the unity of the church, viewed as the body of Christ (1:22–23), as the building or temple of God (2:20–23), and as the bride of Christ (5:23–32). The well-known concluding passage about putting on the armor of God pictures the life of faith as a conflict with evil.

Recommended Readings (passages separated by semicolons indicate chapters; passages separated by colons indicate verses)

The letter to the Ephesians should be read in its entirety.

Philippians

Introductory Overview

Often called "The Personal Epistle," the letter to the Philippians is essentially a note of thanks for favors received while also providing a positive expression of Paul's personal life as a Christian. Also called "The Epistle of Joy," the entire letter exudes Paul's joy and confidence in Christ, even though he is in prison and awaiting trial (1:7).

Philippi was a city in Macedonia, and the Christian community there was the first church established by Paul in Europe (Acts 16:11–13). From the start, Paul's work at Philippi had received opposition, and a main theme of this letter is persistence in faith despite opposition and even the threat of death, which Paul calls following the "mind" of Christ (see 2:2, 5; 3:15; 4:2). The reason for the letter was the presence of Epaphroditus, a member of the church at Philippi who had earlier brought Paul a gift from that church and now was about to return. While Paul was in prison at the time of writing, it is not possible to speak clearly of the time and place. Though the traditional setting is Rome (about 62 CE), it is entirely possible that Paul is writing while imprisoned in Ephesus (55–56 CE); one of Paul's frequent imprisonments (2 Cor. 11:23) may have occurred during his three-year stay at Ephesus (see Acts 20:30), a location much closer to Philippi than Rome. Likewise, the language of Philippians has greater affinity with Paul's earlier "travel epistles" than with later prison epistles such as Philemon or Ephesians and Colossians.

At the center of Philippians is the moving and powerful hymn-like passage that celebrates Christ's humility, self-emptying even to death, and consequent exaltation to lordship (2:6–11). In 3:2–15, Paul provides an insight into his driving passion to achieve the goal for which Christ has called him. In addition, many modern readers connect with this epistle, calling it their favorite book of the Bible. They do so not only for the letter's upbeat tone and message but also for its abundance of inspiring verses, such as 1:20; 3:12–14; 4:6–7, 8, 13, and 19.

Recommended Readings (passages separated by semicolons indicate chapters; passages separated by colons indicate verses)

The letter to the Philippians should be read in its entirety.

Colossians

Introductory Overview

Colossians was written to the church at Colossae (a town in Asia Minor not far from Ephesus), a church not founded by Paul (see 2:1) but likely by his co-worker Epaphras (see 1:7; 4:12). Colossians is closely related to the certainly genuine letter of Philemon, written to the wealthy slaveholder of Onesimus who resided at Colossae (see 4:9) and in whose house the church met for worship. A Prison Epistle (4:10), Colossians is closely related to Ephesians in content, word order, and wording, yet the style, tone, and theological emphasis differ significantly from those of Paul's undisputed letters. While its argumentation is similar to Ephesians, its use of key terms such as "mystery" varies greatly with its meaning in Ephesians. Scholars are divided on how to interpret those differences. Some hold that the letter was written toward the end of Paul's life, presumably at Rome, and that changes in Paul's thinking account for the changes in vocabulary and usage of Paul's undisputed letters. Many scholars disagree, finding compelling reason to conclude that Colossians was not written by Paul but by an anonymous disciple of Paul, to give ongoing authority to the continuing tradition. Ultimately, the letter is part of scripture, and Christians engage it as such.

Paul writes to this church to correct a local heresy that combined certain Jewish ritualistic observances (see 2:16) with features drawn from pagan mythology and philosophy (2:8, 18). The Colossians were seeking the fullness of God (2:9), and they were swayed by false teachers who taught a syncretistic spirituality that combined ascetic practices with esoteric teaching that relied on astrology, angelology, and other "elemental spirits of the universe" (2:8, 20). The false teachers urged that along with worshipping Christ, Christians should also worship angels (2:18), who were seen by them as intermediaries between God and humans. To counter such teaching, Paul does not offer extended arguments against the heresy, but counters with a positive presentation of the person of Christ. In the "Christ Hymn" (1:15–20), the author presents a startling poetic image of the unique lordship of Christ, both throughout the cosmos and in the church. There is no stronger definition of the lordship of Christ in the New Testament.

Recommended Readings (passages separated by semicolons indicate chapters; passages separated by colons indicate verses)

The letter to the Colossians should be read in its entirety.

1 Thessalonians

Introductory Overview

Considered the earliest of Paul's extant letters, this letter was sent by Paul to the church at Thessalonica, a church he had founded recently, shortly after he left Philippi. Written from Corinth about 50 CE (during Paul's second missionary journey), 1 Thessalonians encourages believers who are experiencing persecution for their faith. Paul's co-worker Timothy had recently arrived from Thessalonica, bringing with him two urgent questions requiring an immediate answer. Some of the Thessalonians were perplexed by the death of believers, and wondered whether those who had died would be excluded from the general resurrection of the dead, an event they expected in the near future.

The main theme of 1 Thessalonians, found in chapters 4 and 5, concerns the second coming of Christ (called the Parousia), and the Thessalonians wish to know the fate of those who die before the Parousia, as well as the date of that event. Concerning the fate, Paul replies with an apocalyptic narrative, which makes clear that at the second coming, all believers "will be with the Lord forever" (4:13–18). [Incidentally, the Parousia should not be confused with popular notions of a secret rapture, which has no biblical basis. First century believers did not anticipate removal from this earth in the end time, but rather Christ's coming to establish a "millennial kingdom" on earth.] Regarding the date of the Parousia, Paul refuses to give a specific answer, only to remind them of what he had taught them in person and to exhort them to remain alert, for the return would be sudden and unexpected, like "a thief in the night: (5:1–11).

Recommended Readings (passages separated by semicolons indicate chapters; passages separated by colons indicate verses)

Chapters 3:11–5:28

2 Thessalonians

Introductory Overview

This letter continues the theme of 1 Thessalonians, although it provides radically different answers to their questions concerning the Parousia. According to 2 Thessalonians, the Parousia will be a time of judgment and vindication, bringing rest for believers who have suffered and vengeance upon unbelievers (1:5–10). Whereas in 1 Thessalonians Paul had refused to give a specific answer regarding the date of the Parousia, in 2 Thessalonians he changes his mind, providing a detailed timeline of end-time events. In 1 Thessalonians, readers sense that the expectation of the end is imminent, but in 2 Thessalonians readers learn that the end would not come suddenly or soon, and that believers should focus on the proper conduct of their lives (3:6–13). On account of differences in style, setting, and eschatology between the two Thessalonian letters, the majority of biblical scholars now conclude that 2 Thessalonians was written by a later anonymous disciple of Paul who wished to update Paul's teaching on the Parousia.

Recommended Readings (passages separated by semicolons indicate chapters; passages separated by colons indicate verses)

Chapters 1–3

Chapter 8

NEW TESTAMENT LITERATURE, PART II
Overview and Passages

THIS CHAPTER, THE SECOND on the books of the New Testament, provides a brief introduction to four letters attributed to Paul, the General Epistles, and the book of Revelation, each in literary sequence (namely, in biblical order). Each introductory overview is followed by a list of recommended readings from that book of the Bible. A complete guide of daily readings, designed to lead individuals through the sixty-six books of the Bible (plus several of the apocryphal/deuterocanonical books) in eleven months or less, is provided in the appendix to this book.

1 Timothy

Introductory Overview

The two letters to Timothy, along with the one to Titus, are commonly called the Pastoral Epistles because they are addressed to two associates of Paul who have become pastors of churches. First Timothy has a twofold purpose: to provide guidance to a young pastor regarding church administration and to oppose false teaching. Judging by differences in style, vocabulary, and theology from Paul's undisputed letters, most modern scholars attribute the Pastorals to a later disciple of Paul, written to present Paul's teaching to a later and different setting, using it as a bulwark against wrong teaching and practice. Some scholars believe that fragments of Paul's writings are included in the Pastorals, while others hold that the personal greetings and remarks are inserted to give Paul's authority to the teachings of these letters.

In 1 Timothy, the author offers suggestions for the regulation of public worship, defines the position of men and women in the community, lays down the qualifications of bishops and deacons, warns against false teachers, and concludes with various moral exhortations. Given changes in setting and church administration from Paul's earlier letters, 1 Timothy, like Titus, were likely written about 100–110 CE, decades after the death of Paul.

Recommended Readings (passages separated by semicolons indicate chapters; passages separated by colons indicate verses)

Chapters 2:1–7; 4:1–10; 6:6–21

2 Timothy

Introductory Overview

The most personal of the Pastorals, 2 Timothy is the closest to Paul's style and thought of the Pastorals and has the best claim to authenticity. Focusing on the theme of faithful endurance, it presents Paul's farewell message. Some scholars claim it was dictated to a scribe, to whom Paul gave great freedom in composition. Others believe it was composed toward the end of the first century by a devoted follower of Paul, who utilized several fragments or shorter letters by Paul. If 2 Timothy is authentic, it would have been written from Rome (1:17), where Paul is a prisoner (1:8; 2:9), possibly for a second time. Paul is expecting to be executed soon (4:6), and being alone, he longs for Timothy to be with him at the end (4:21). Here and in passages such as 4:6–18, we hear the voice of the apostle.

Recommended Readings (passages separated by semicolons indicate chapters; passages separated by colons indicate verses)

2 Timothy should be read in its entirety.

Titus

Introductory Overview

The teaching of Titus strongly parallels that of 1 Timothy, and like that letter, is made up of general teaching regarding sound doctrine. Although Titus is not mentioned in the book of Acts, he appears as an important companion of Paul in Galatians and in 2 Corinthians. Titus, a Greek was probably one of the first Gentile Christians. In Galatians 2:1–3 we learn that Titus accompanied Paul to Jerusalem when the latter's apostleship was recognized by the early Christian leaders in Jerusalem. If Paul and Titus traveled to Crete, as the letter to Titus presupposes (1:5), this may have been as part of the visit to Greece mentioned in Acts 20:3 or possibly at a later time, if Paul was released from his first Roman imprisonment, with which Acts 28 closes. Like 1 Timothy, the letter to Titus sets forth what is required of leaders in the church (chapter 1). The letter also emphasizes the duties of various classes in society, such as older men, older women, younger men, and slaves (chapter 2), and closes with the responsibility of believers in the world, admonishing them to avoid theoretical debates while focusing on humility, gentleness, obedience, and courtesy, qualities made possible by God's mercy in Christ (chapter 3)

Recommended Readings (passages separated by semicolons indicate chapters; passages separated by colons indicate verses)

Due to its parallels with 1 Timothy and to many admonitions that no longer seem applicable in a pluralistic society, this letter may be skipped in its entirety.

Philemon

Introductory Overview

The most personal of all Paul's letters, Philemon was likely written during Paul's imprisonment at Rome (61–63). Philemon was a leading member of the church at Colossae, whose slave Onesimus had likely run away or at least proven useless to Philemon. In this letter, Paul's shortest, Paul asks Philemon to receive Onesimus, now a fellow Christian, without punishment. As in his other letters, Paul does not speak against the institution of slavery, but his plea for love and mercy in this letter shows how Christian ways were changing old harsh customs, though it would take a long time before slavery was ended.

Recommended Readings (passages separated by semicolons indicate chapters; passages separated by colons indicate verses)

Philemon should be read in its entirety.

THE GENERAL (CATHOLIC) EPISTLES

Classified with James and letters attributed to Peter, John, and Jude as General or Catholic Epistles, Hebrews, together with the other General Letters, is addressed not to a single individual or Christian community but to a cluster of congregations. The General Epistles are less like personal letters and more like official letters (epistles) or sermons from a bishop or elder to a group of churches. It is possible to divide these letters into two overarching themes: three letters help readers understand the early church's Jewish heritage (Hebrews, James, and 1 Peter), and five with the perils of heresies (2 Peter, the three epistles of John, and Jude).

Hebrews

Introductory Overview

Long ascribed to Paul, Hebrews is an anonymous treatise on the preeminence of Jesus Christ. The longest sustained argument of any book in the Bible, Hebrews was written to Jewish Christians who were on the point of returning to Judaism, perhaps because of persecution. In order to win them back to the Christian faith, the author emphasizes three points: (1) the superiority of Jesus Christ over Old Testament figures such as prophets, angels, and the lawgiver Moses (chapters 1–3); (2) the superiority of Christ's priesthood over the priesthood of Aaron (chapters 4–7); and (3) the superiority of Christ's sacrifice of himself over the Levitical sacrifices (chapters 8–10).

While insisting on the humanity of Jesus (see 2:14–18; 4:15), the focus of Hebrews is not earthly or historical matters but on the saving significance of Jesus' death and resurrection. The epistle concludes with an exhortation on faith (11:1–3), including the famous roll call of the faithful (11:4–40) and a call to faithfulness, hospitality, and obedience, modeled on the pioneering work of Jesus Christ (chapters 12–13). A sermon or treatise sent as a letter, Hebrews is very different in its literary style and theological conception from Paul's letters. Possibly addressed to discouraged Jewish Christians at Rome during the reign of Nero, Hebrews is notoriously difficult to date, and may have been written anytime between 60 and 100 CE.

Recommended Readings (passages separated by semicolons indicate chapters; passages separated by colons indicate verses)

Chapters 1–2; 4:12–7:28; 11:1–12:2

James

Introductory Overview

An elegantly composed treatise, James contains numerous exhortations, most of them parallel to directives found in Jewish wisdom traditions. While it begins with an epistolary greeting, James lacks other formal characteristics of a letter. The central section contains three discourses, the first on partiality (2:1–13), the second on faith and works (2:14–26), and the last on speech (3:1–12). Its emphasis on behavior rather than on doctrine have led some readers to question whether James is uniquely Christian. Other than two references to Jesus (1:1; 2:1), most of the teaching in James is common to other Hellenistic wisdom literature of the day.

Jesus, it seems, valued the Jewish Law, and the letter of James continued this theme: it emphasizes that religious belief is worthless if it does not affect the way people live. What God considers to be pure and genuine religion is this: "to care for orphans and widows in their distress, and to keep oneself unstained by the world" (Jas 1:27). The heart of real devotion to God is to love one's neighbor as oneself (2:1–13). Like Jesus, James uses illustrations to deliver his message, many from the familiar world of Palestinian agriculture. While the epistle of James, like Jesus' Sermon on the Mount, lacks any coherent argument as such, its message is not lost on its readers. People who endure suffering patiently, trusting in God for deliverance, will be vindicated in the end (Jas 5:7–20).

Though the letter is attributed to James, the brother of Jesus and a leader in the Jerusalem church from 36 CE until his martyrdom in 62, the author is anonymous and may, like many other books of the Bible, put his work under the patronage of a revered figure. In the New Testament, the figure of James is associated with the dispute over "faith and works."

New Testament Literature, Part II

While Paul would certainly agree with James that the Christian life should be expressed by deeds of love (see Gal 5:6), James appears to be opposed to a distorted form of Paulinism, which emphasizes faith to the neglect of obligation to aid those in need (2:14–26). Due to its style and lack of historical markers, no scholarly consensus has been reached on its date or provenance, though a post-Pauline date seems most compelling. James is not addressed to a specific church; instead, it appears to be a general letter written to numerous diaspora churches scattered abroad (see 1:1).

Recommended Readings (passages separated by semicolons indicate chapters; passages separated by colons indicate verses)

Chapters 1–4

1 Peter

Introductory Overview

According to tradition, the apostle Peter wrote this letter from Rome, perhaps after the outbreak of the persecution by the emperor Nero in 64. Although 1 Peter claims to be written by the disciple of Jesus, Simon Peter, this is highly unlikely, given the fact that Peter was a lower-class Jewish fisherman from Galilee, whereas this book is written by a well-educated, rhetorically trained Greek-speaking Christian. Although it is possible that Peter wrote the book or dictated its contents to someone (perhaps the "Silvanus" mentioned in 5:12), who translated his words into Greek and provided them with a rhetorical flourish, it is more likely that the book was written pseudonymously in Peter's name, as were several other books that have come down to us from the second century, such as the gospel of Peter, three apocalypses attributed to Peter, several "Acts" of Peter, and other Petrine letters. Though 1 Peter was accepted as canonical at an early date, many scholars prefer a date about 100 CE.

First Peter, it seems, is a kind of circular letter addressed to Christians scattered throughout several of the provinces of Asia Minor who are experiencing harsh forms of suffering through persecution. The author urges them not to suffer for any wrongdoing but only for doing what is right. In particular, they should willingly and fearlessly suffer, if suffer they must, for the sake of their Christian faith. Although written in the name of the apostle Peter, the letter was written by one of his disciples in Rome. The letter lacks the kind of material one would expect from an eyewitness. Instead, the letter reflects much of the language and thought of the Pauline letters, and doubtless combines Petrine and Pauline traditions. By the end of the first century, the church at Rome found itself the heir of both Peter and Paul, and the custodian of the traditions associated with each. A late date for the letter is also suggested by the use of the term "Babylon" (5:13) as a designation for Rome, which became current only after 70 CE. Except for the first word, the letter makes no claim to authorship by an apostle, but specifically indicates that the author was an elder (5:1).

Given the curious matter of baptism in 3:18–22, in the past some scholars argued that the central portion of the letter (1:3–4:11) may have been taken from an early service of baptism, though this view is now largely rejected for lack of evidence. The expression "he descended into hell" found in the Apostles' Creed is said to have come from 3:19, which may mean that Christ announced his saving work in the realm of the dead to the unrepentant who died as a result of the flood in Noah's day. First Peter concludes with miscellaneous matters, notably with a statement on the meaning of suffering (4:12–19).

Recommended Readings (passages separated by semicolons indicate chapters; passages separated by colons indicate verses)

Chapters 1–2; 4:8–5:11

2 Peter and Jude

Introductory Overview

Second Peter and Jude are the two most disputed books of the New Testament in terms of authorship. Both books may have originated from a group of Peter's disciples, much like the Johannine letters originated from a group or "school" of John's disciples. Second Peter was written later than 1 Peter and by a different author. The end of the first century, like the start of the second, witnessed the emergence of various groups who, at a later date, came to be regarded as heretical or heterodox, and it is these groups and their views that ultimately lost the argument. It is no surprise that the last books of the New Testament to be written have as their main theme warnings and arguments against heretical teachings and practices. Whether by "heresies" we refer to moral or doctrinal deviancy, the opponents attacked in this group of letters all appear to be active in Asia Minor around the same time.

New Testament Literature, Part II

The influence of false teachers is the subject of Jude and 2 Peter. These books clearly belong together, for almost the whole of Jude (in slightly modified form) is contained in 2 Peter (compare 2:1–8 with Jude 4–16). Although the author of 2 Peter calls himself "Simon Peter, a servant and apostle of Jesus Christ" (1:1), and makes reference to his being present at the transfiguration of Jesus (1:18), his style and contents have led modern scholars to regard it as the work of an unknown author of the early second century. Unlike the style of 1 Peter, which is written in fluent koine Greek, the style of 2 Peter has been described as "pseudo-literary"; its wording is unusual, artificial, and often obscure, and according to Bruce Metzger, is "the one book in the New Testament which gains by translation."[1]

Second Peter's style and content point to a date long after Peter's lifetime. Two passages point to a late date: 3:3–4 indicates that the apostolic age is over, and 3:16 indicates that the letters of Paul have been collected and are being referred to as "scripture." Both Jude and 2 Peter hit heresy hard, yielding no compromise. This emphasis points to a period of doctrinal struggle threatening the church's unity. It would take at least two centuries before orthodox Christianity achieved doctrinal and political authority.

Taking the form of a farewell letter written by the apostle Peter (1:12–15) and addressed to all Christians, 2 Peter begins as an exhortation to maintain holiness of character, followed by a warning (based on the letter of Jude) against heresy, which is viewed as leading to immorality. The letter concludes with a reminder of the Parousia, a hope for the coming of Christ that some individuals at that time had begun to ridicule (3:3–4). Because the author refers to the letters of Paul as "scripture" (4:16), a term apparently not applied to them until long after Paul's death, most modern scholars think that this letter was composed in Peter's name sometime between 100 and 150 CE.

Like 2 Peter, the purpose of Jude was to combat doctrines that were being spread by heretical teachers. Using examples drawn from the Old Testament and containing references to two Jewish pseudepigraphic books (Enoch and the Assumption of Moses), the author graphically illustrates the danger of false teaching. Jude's date and destination cannot be determined with precision, though it clearly predates 2 Peter, whose author duplicates arguments in Jude 3–18. That 2 Peter used Jude and not the reverse is supported by the absence from 2 Peter of a passage in Jude 9, taken from the Assumption of Moses, for it seems more likely that 2 Peter omitted the

---

1. Metzger, *New Testament*, 258.

reference than that Jude added it. Writing in the late first or early second century to Christians everywhere, the author identified himself as one of the brothers of Jesus (see Matt 13:55; Mark 6:3) to lend authority to his appeal for integrity and unity. Jude ends with a moving benediction (1:24–25).

Recommended Readings (passages separated by semicolons indicate chapters; passages separated by colons indicate verses)

Second Peter 3; Jude 1:24–25

1–3 John

Introductory Overview

The three letters of John give us a fascinating glimpse into the life of the Christian church in Asia Minor toward the close of the first century. There appears to have been a school of Christian thought at this time organized around a man known as John the elder, who himself may have been a disciple of John, son of Zebedee, which opens up the possibility that the Johannine literature (the gospel, the three epistles, and the book of Revelation), are the products of different members of that Johannine school. If that is so, it would account for the similarities found in these works as well as for the obvious differences.

The form of 1 John differs markedly from that of 2 and 3 John. The latter two are clearly letters, while 1 John lacks the usual features of a letter. The document appears to be an anthology of loosely related admonitions, possibly sermonic fragments, strung together into written form. Though the structure of 1 John remains obscure, its message revolves around five themes: (1) the fleshly humanity of Christ (4:2); (2) the saving work of Christ (1:7, 9; 2:2; 3:5; 4:10); (3) the understanding of sin (1:8, 10; 3:4, 8, 9; 5:16–17); (4) the importance of moral living (1:7; 2:3, 4, 6, 24; 3:7, 14; 4:5, 6, 16), based upon the commandment to "love one another" (3:11, 23; 4:7, 11–12); and (5) the "last days" (2:18, 28; 3:2; 4:17, 18). Some of these themes appear in 2 and 3 John as well.

While we are limited in our knowledge of the setting out of which and for which 1 John was written, it seems clear that a group once within a church (or churches) has withdrawn, and its members—in the view of the Johannine author—were never full participants or even authentic Christians (2:19). The differences between the author of 1 John and the separatists seem to center on proper views of Christ, sin, and morality. It appears that 1 John was written to strengthen the confidence of the original Johannine churches. The author wants to solidify the readers into a coherent group around a single understanding of Christian life and belief.

The setting for 1 John is related to that of 2 John, whose author urges the readers to lead moral lives, perhaps in contrast to the dissidents (verses 5–6). These dissenters are propagating their views in nearby congregations, and the "elder" is attempting to defuse their influence. Like 1 John, 2 John also counsels a view of Christ as a fleshly being, against "deceivers" who teach otherwise (verse 7). Such false Christians should be denied hospitality when they arrive (verse 10).

Third John presents a different setting, a power struggle between rivals within a congregation. A certain Diotrephes has proven himself an irritant in the congregation of which Gaius (the recipient of the letter) is a leader. An isolationist who views himself a purist, Diotrephes refuses to recognize the authority of the elder and gossips about his leadership (verse 10). He has driven off those who disagree with him and is refusing even to welcome Christian visitors. The elder in this case tries to win the loyalty of Gaius and thereby strengthen the author's influence in the congregation.

These three documents are important in the New Testament for they present a Christian community struggling between doctrinal and ethical purity on the one hand and tolerance on the other. The twin issues of orthodoxy and authority are paramount in the emergence of the church. If the letters of John were written after the gospel of John, which is dated 90–95 CE, they are believed to have appeared between 100–110. While the gospel of John may come from a different hand, it seems likely that the three letters have a common authorship.

Recommended Readings (passages separated by semicolons indicate chapters; passages separated by colons indicate verses)

While 1 John should be read in its entirety, 2 and 3 John may be skipped in their entirety.

Revelation

Introductory Overview

The book of Revelation, also called the Apocalypse of John, is a fitting close to the Old and New Testament, for its final chapters depict the consummation toward which the entire biblical message is focused. Revelation may be described as an inspired picture-book that, by an accumulation of magnificent poetic imagery, makes a powerful appeal to the reader's imagination. Many of the details of its pictures are intended to contribute to the total impression, and are not to be isolated and interpreted with detached literalism.

As is the case with many biblical books, we know nothing about the author except for what we can infer from the book itself, namely, that the author was an early Christian prophet named John. In every chapter, John's visions are informed by the traditions and images of the Old Testament. As a thoroughly apocalyptic document, the book of Revelation is unique in the New Testament but has much in common with parts of Old Testament books such as Daniel, Isaiah, and Zechariah. In addition, its language and structure seem strongly influence by Ezekiel.

An important way to read Revelation is to understand its cumulative or even progressive nature; thus read, the book involves a series of parallel sections that depict the struggle of the church and its victory over evil through God's providence. There are probably seven of these sections, although only five are clearly marked. Bracketed by a prologue (1:1–8) and an epilogue (22:6–21), the seven parallel sections include a vision of the church imperfect in the world (1:9-3:22); five parallel sections consisting of a scroll with seven seals (4:1–8:1); seven trumpets (8:2–11:19); seven actions (chapters 12–14); seven bowls (chapters 15–16); and seven final judgments (171–21:8); followed by a vision of the church perfect in glory (21:9–22:5). Throughout these sections, three things progress and increase simultaneously: (1) increase of evil, (2) increasing severity of judgment, and (3) perfecting of the faithful church.

While Revelation can be understood in a number of ways, there are four traditional schools of interpretation: (1) the *preterist approach* takes a historical view, stressing the importance of the original setting to determine the meaning of the text (hope for the end of the ungodly and totalitarian Roman empire); (2) the *idealist approach* uses a symbolic interpretation to depict the eternal conflict of good and evil; (3) the *historicist approach* views the book as a chronological presentation of the entire course of church history (chapters 2-3 are regarded as addressing the church of John's time and chapters 8-22 are interpreted as predicting all future history); and (4) the *futurist approach*, which considers the visions of chapters 4–22 as yet to be fulfilled.

New Testament Literature, Part II

Despite using apocalyptic hyperbole and fervor, the book's underlying message is of hope, not of fear. In Revelation, the outcome of history is assumed; because God reigns, hope is forever near. To understand the message of Revelation, readers must continually take into consideration the book's goal in 22:5: "I am making all things new." According to the Bible, the arc of history is bent toward hope.

Recommended Readings (passages separated by semicolons indicate chapters; passages separated by colons indicate verses)

Chapters 1–6; 12–14; 19–22

APPENDIX

Reading the (Abridged) Bible in Less than a Year: Daily Readings

JANUARY

1. Genesis 1–2
2. Genesis 3–4
3. Genesis 6–7
4. Genesis 8:1–9:17
5. Genesis 11:1–9; 11:27–13:18
6. Genesis 14–15
7. Genesis 16–17
8. Genesis 18–19
9. Genesis 20–21
10. Genesis 22–23
11. Genesis 24:1–25:11
12. Genesis 25:19–34; 27:1–46
13. Genesis 28–29
14. Genesis 30–31
15. Genesis 32–33
16. Genesis 35 and 37
17. Genesis 39–40
18. Genesis 41–42
19. Genesis 43–45
20. Genesis 47–48
21. Genesis 49–50
22. Exodus 1–2
23. Exodus 3:1–4:20
24. Exodus 4:27–6:13
25. Exodus 7:8–8:32
26. Exodus 9–10
27. Exodus 11:1–12:42
28. Exodus 13:17–15:27
29. Exodus 16–17
30. Exodus 18–19
31. Exodus 20–21

APPENDIX

FEBRUARY

1. Exodus 22–23
2. Exodus 24–25; 28:1–5
3. Exodus 31:18–33:23
4. Exodus 34; 40
5. Numbers 10:11–11:35
6. Numbers 12–13
7. Numbers 14
8. Numbers 20–21
9. Numbers 22–24
10. Numbers 26:63–27:23
11. Deuteronomy 1–2
12. Deuteronomy 3–4
13. Deuteronomy 5–6
14. Deuteronomy 18:9–22; 27:9–26
15. Deuteronomy 28
16. Deuteronomy 29–30; 34
17. Joshua 1–3
18. Joshua 4–6
19. Joshua 7–9
20. Joshua 10–11
21. Joshua 21:41–24:33
22. Judges 1–3
23. Judges 4–5
24. Judges 6–7
25. Judges 8–9
26. Judges 10–11
27. Judges 12–14
28. Judges 15–16

MARCH

1. Ruth 1–2
2. Ruth 3–4
3. 1 Samuel 1–2
4. 1 Samuel 3–4
5. 1 Samuel 5–7
6. 1 Samuel 8–9
7. 1 Samuel 10–11
8. 1 Samuel 13–14
9. 1 Samuel 15–16
10. 1 Samuel 17-18
11. 1 Samuel 19–20
12. 1 Samuel 21–22
13. 1 Samuel 23–24
14. 1 Samuel 25
15. 1 Samuel 26–27
16. 1 Samuel 28–29
17. 1 Samuel 30–31
18. 2 Samuel 1–2
19. 2 Samuel 3–4
20. 2 Samuel 5–6
21. 2 Samuel 7–9
22. 2 Samuel 11–12
23. 2 Samuel 13–14
24. 2 Samuel 15–16
25. 2 Samuel 17–18
26. 2 Samuel 19–22
27. 2 Samuel 23:1–7; 24
28. 1 Kings 1
29. 1 Kings 2
30. 1 Kings 3–5
31. 1 Kings 6–7

APPENDIX

APRIL

1. 1 Kings 8
2. 1 Kings 9–10
3. 1 Kings 11–12
4. 1 Kings 13–14
5. 1 Kings 17–18
6. 1 Kings 19–20
7. 1 Kings 21–22
8. 2 Kings 1:1–2:15
9. 2 Kings 4–5
10. 2 Kings 6–7
11. 2 Kings 8–9
12. 2 Kings 10–11
13. 2 Kings 12–13
14. 2 Kings 17–18
15. 2 Kings 19–21
16. 2 Kings 22–23
17. 2 Kings 25–25
18. 2 Chronicles 35:20–36:23
19. Ezra 1; 3:1–4:5
20. Ezra 5–7; 8:15–36
21. Nehemiah 8; Ezra 9:1–10:17
22. Nehemiah 1–2; 4
23. Nehemiah 5:1–7:4
24. Esther 1–3
25. Esther 4–6
26. Esther 7–10
27. Job 1–3
28. Job 28–30
29. Job 31–33
30. Job 34–37

MAY

1. Job 38–39
2. Job 40–42
3. Psalm 1; 2; 5; 6
4. Psalm 8; 13–16
5. Psalm 18–19
6. Psalm 22–24
7. Psalm 27; 29; 30
8. Psalm 32; 33; 37
9. Psalm 39–41
10. Psalm 42–43; 45–46
11. Psalm 49; 51; 55
12. Psalm 61; 62; 63; 65
13. Psalm 67; 69; 72
14. Psalm 73; 78
15. Psalm 82; 84; 87; 88
16. Psalm 89
17. Psalm 90–92
18. Psalm 95–98
19. Psalm 100; 102–104
20. Psalm 107–108
21. Psalm 110; 111; 114; 116
22. Psalm 117–118; 119:1–20, 105–112, 129–136, 161–176
23. Psalm 121–123; 127–128
24. Psalm 130–131; 133; 139
25. Psalm 144; 145; 148; 150
26. Proverbs 1–2
27. Proverbs 3–4
28. Proverbs 5–6
29. Proverbs 7–9
30. Proverbs 31:10–31
31. Ecclesiastes 1–2

APPENDIX

JUNE

1. Ecclesiastes 3–4
2. Ecclesiastes 5–6
3. Ecclesiastes 7–8
4. Ecclesiastes 9; 11–12
5. Wisdom 1–2
6. Wisdom 3; 6:12–25
7. Wisdom 7
8. Wisdom 8–9
9. Sirach 1; 24; 51
10. Song of Solomon 2:1–4; 8:6–7; Tobit 1–3
11. Tobit 4–6
12. Tobit 7–9
13. Tobit 10–12
14. Tobit 13–14
15. Isaiah 1:1–2:5
16. Isaiah 5–6
17. Isaiah 7–9
18. Isaiah 11–12
19. Isaiah 25–26
20. Isaiah 27–28
21. Isaiah 29:13–24
22. Isaiah 30:8–31:9
23. Isaiah 32–33
24. Isaiah 35; 39
25. Isaiah 40–41
26. Isaiah 42–43
27. Isaiah 44–45
28. Isaiah 49–50
29. Isaiah 51:1–52:12
30. Isaiah 52:13–55:13

JULY

1. Isaiah 56; 58
2. Isaiah 59–61
3. Isaiah 62–64
4. Isaiah 65–66
5. Jeremiah 1–2
6. Jeremiah 3–4
7. Jeremiah 7:1–29
8. Jeremiah 8:18–9:24
9. Jeremiah 11–12
10. Jeremiah 13:1–14:16
11. Jeremiah 15:5–16:21
12. Jeremiah 17:1–18:12
13. Jeremiah 19–21
14. Jeremiah 22–23
15. Jeremiah 24–26
16. Jeremiah 27–28
17. Jeremiah 29–30
18. Jeremiah 31–32
19. Jeremiah 33–34
20. Jeremiah 36–37
21. Jeremiah 38–40
22. Jeremiah 41–43
23. Jeremiah 50
24. Jeremiah 51:1–58; 52:28–34
25. Lamentations 1; 2:13–15; 3:1–6, 16–18, 22–23
26. Ezekiel 1–2
27. Ezekiel 3–5
28. Ezekiel 8–9; 11:14–25
29. Ezekiel 12–14
30. Ezekiel 15–16
31. Ezekiel 17–18

Appendix

AUGUST

1. Ezekiel 24; 33:21–34:31
2. Ezekiel 36:22–37:28
3. Ezekiel 39:1–40:4
4. Ezekiel 47:1–12, 21–23; 48:30–35
5. Daniel 1–2
6. Daniel 3–4
7. Daniel 5–6
8. Daniel 7; 12:1–4
9. Hosea 1–3
10. Hosea 4:1–6:6
11. Hosea 9:1–10:6; 11; 14
12. Joel 1:1–3:3; 3:13–21
13. Amos 1:1–2; 3:1–8; 5:1–24
14. Amos 7:10–9:6
15. Jonah 1–4
16. Micah 1:1; 4:11–5:4; 6:1–8; 7:14–20
17. Habakkuk 1–3
18. Zephaniah 1:1–3; 3:1–20
19. Haggai 1:1–2:9; 2:20–23
20. Zechariah 1–3
21. Zechariah 4–6
22. Zechariah 9:9–10:12; 12:10–14:21
23. Malachi 1; 3; 4
24. Mark 1–2
25. Mark 3–4
26. Mark 5–6
27. Mark 7–8
28. Mark 9
29. Mark 10
30. Mark 11–12
31. Mark 13–14

SEPTEMBER

1. Mark 15–16
2. Matthew 1:18–2:23
3. Matthew 5
4. Matthew 6–7
5. Matthew 12:38–45; 18:1–19:2
6. Matthew 20:1–19; 21:1–32
7. Matthew 23:1–39; 25:1–13
8. Matthew 25:31–26:16; 27:15–32
9. Matthew 27:33–28:20
10. Luke 1
11. Luke 2:1–3:22
12. Luke 4:1–30; 7:1–35
13. Luke 9:51–10:42
14. Luke 11:37–12:21; 13:1–17
15. Luke 13:31–15:32
16. Luke 16:1–18:14
17. Luke 19:1–48; 21:5–36
18. Luke 22:54–23:56
19. Luke 24
20. John 1
21. John 2–3
22. John 4–5
23. John 6
24. John 7
25. John 8–9
26. John 10–11
27. John 12–13
28. John 14–15
29. John 16–17
30. John 18–19

Appendix

OCTOBER

1. John 20–21
2. Acts 1–2
3. Acts 3–4
4. Acts 5–6
5. Acts 7:1–2a; 7:48–8:40
6. Acts 9–10
7. Acts 11–12
8. Acts 13–14
9. Acts 15–16
10. Acts 17–18
11. Acts 19–20
12. Acts 21–22
13. Acts 23:1–25:12
14. Acts 27–28
15. Romans 1
16. Romans 2–3
17. Romans 5–6
18. Romans 8–9
19. Romans 10–11
20. Romans 12–14
21. 1 Corinthians 1–2
22. 1 Corinthians 3; 9
23. 1 Corinthians 12:1–14:5
24. 1 Corinthians 15
25. 2 Corinthians 1–2
26. 2 Corinthians 3–5
27. 2 Corinthians 10:1–12:10
28. Galatians 1–2
29. Galatians 3–4
30. Galatians 5–6
31. Ephesians 1–2

NOVEMBER

1. Ephesians 3–4
2. Ephesians 5–6
3. Philippians 1–2
4. Philippians 3–4
5. Colossians 1–2
6. Colossians 3–4
7. 1 Thessalonians 3:11–5:28
8. 2 Thessalonians 1–3
9. 1 Timothy 2:1–7; 4:1–10; 6:6–21
10. 2 Timothy 1–2
11. 2 Timothy 3–4
12. Philemon 1:1–25
13. Hebrews 1–2
14. Hebrews 4:12–5:14
15. Hebrews 6–7
16. Hebrews 11:1–12:2
17. James 1–2
18. James 3–4
19. 1 Peter 1–2
20. 1 Peter 4:8–5:11
21. 2 Peter 3; Jude 1:24–25
22. 1 John 1–2
23. 1 John 3–5
24. Revelation 1–2
25. Revelation 3–4
26. Revelation 5–6
27. Revelation 12–13
28. Revelation 14
29. Revelation 19–20
30. Revelation 21–22

Bibliography

Achtemeier, Paul J. *The Inspiration of Scripture: Problems and Proposals.* Philadelphia: Westminster, 1980.
Anderson, Bernhard W. *Contours of Old Testament Theology.* Minneapolis: Fortress, 1999.
———. *Understanding the Old Testament.* 5th ed. Upper Saddle River, NJ: Pearson Prentice Hall, 2007.
———. *The Unfolding Drama of the Bible.* 4th ed. Minneapolis: Fortress, 2006.
Borg, Marcus J. *The God We Never Knew.* San Francisco: HarperSanFrancisco, 1998.
———. *The Heart of Christianity.* San Francisco: HarperSanFrancisco, 2004.
———. *Meeting Jesus Again for the First Time.* San Francisco: HarperSanFrancisco, 1994.
———. *Reading the Bible Again for the First Time.* San Francisco: HarperSanFrancisco, 2001.
Brown, Raymond E. *An Introduction to the New Testament.* San Francisco: Doubleday, 1997.
Brown, Raymond E., et al. *The New Jerome Biblical Commentary.* Upper Saddle River, NJ: Prentice Hall, 1990.
Bruce, F. F. *The New Testament Development of Old Testament Themes.* Grand Rapids, Eerdmans, 1968.
———. *Paul, Apostle of the Heart Set Free.* Grand Rapids: Eerdmans, 1991.
Childs, Brevard. *Biblical Theology in Crisis.* Philadelphia: Westminster, 1970.
———. *Biblical Theology of the Old and New Testaments.* Minneapolis: Fortress, 1977.
———. *Introduction to the Old Testament as Scripture.* Philadelphia: Fortress, 1979.
Coogan, Michael D. *A Brief Introduction to the Old Testament.* New York: Oxford University Press, 2009.
Cory, Catherine. *A Voyage through the New Testament.* Upper Saddle River, NJ: Pearson Prentice Hall, 2008.
Countryman, L. William. *Biblical Authority or Biblical Tyranny? Scripture and the Christian Pilgrimage.* Valley Forge: PA: Trinity International, 1994.
Drane, John. *Introducing the New Testament.* Revised and Updated. Minneapolis: Fortress, 2001.
Ehrman, Bart D. *A Brief Introduction to the New Testament.* 3rd ed. New York: Oxford University Press, 2013.
———. *The New Testament: A Historical Introduction to the Early Christian Writings.* 7th ed. New York: Oxford University Press, 2020.
Hendricks, Howard G., and William D. *Living by the Book: The Art and Science of Reading the Bible.* Chicago: Moody, 2007.

Bibliography

McLaren, Brian. *Faith After Doubt: Why Your Beliefs Stopped Working and What to Do About It*. New York: St. Martin's, 2021.

Metzger, Bruce M. *The New Testament: Its Background, Growth, and Content*. Nashville, TN: Abingdon, 1965.

———. *The Reader's Digest Bible*. Pleasantville, NY: The Reader's Digest Association, 1982.

Metzger, Bruce M., and Michael D. Coogan. *The Oxford Guide to Ideas & Issues of the Bible*. New York: Oxford University Press, 2001.

Neill, Stephen. *Jesus Through Many Eyes: Introduction to the Theology of the New Testament*. Philadelphia: Fortress, 1976.

Ryken, Leland. *How to Read the Bible as Literature*. Grand Rapids, MI: Zondervan, 1984.

Spong, John Shelby. *Liberating the Gospels: Reading the Bible with Jewish Eyes*. San Francisco: HarperSanFrancisco, 1996.

———. *Rescuing the Bible from Fundamentalism*. San Francisco: HarperSanFrancisco, 1991.

———. *The Sins of Scripture*. San Francisco: HarperOne, 2006.

Vande Kappelle, Robert P. *Beyond Belief: Faith, Science, and the Value of Unknowing*. Eugene: OR: Wipf & Stock, 2012.

———. *Dark Splendor: Spiritual Fitness for the Second Half of Life*. Eugene, OR: Wipf & Stock, 2015.

———. *Holistic Happiness; Spirituality and a Healing Lifestyle*. Eugene, OR: Wipf & Stock, 2022.

———. *Outgrowing Cultic Christianity: Restoring the Role of Religion*. Eugene, OR: Wipf & Stock, 2021.

———. *Refined by Fire: Rethinking Essential Teachings in Scripture*. Eugene, OR: Wipf & Stock, 2018.

———. *Securing Life: The Enduring Message of the Bible*. Eugene, OR: Wipf & Stock, 2016.

———. *Understanding Scripture: Forty Things to Know about the Christian Bible*. Eugene, OR: Wipf & Stock, 2020.

Virkler, Henry A., and Karelynne Gerber Ayayo. *Hermeneutics: Principles and Processes of Biblical Interpretation*. 2nd ed. Grand Rapids, MI: Baker, 2007.

Walls, Andrew F. *The Cross-Cultural Process in Christian History*. Maryknoll, NY: Orbis, 2002.

———. *The Missionary Movement in Christian History: Studies in the Transmission of Faith*. Maryknoll, NY: Orbis, 1996.

Yancey, Philip, and Brenda Quinn. *Meet the Bible*. Grand Rapids, MI: Zondervan, 2000.

Index

Acts, book of, 9, 10, 11, 22, 31, 43, 91, 95, 98, 99, 101, 104–5, 108, 110, 116
afterlife, 14, 26, 45
Agassiz, Louis, 49
American Standard Version, 65, 67
Amos, book of, 6, 7, 86, 90, 91–92, 95
apocalypse, apocalyptic, 9, 11, 50, 53, 89, 91, 96, 97, 104, 112, 124, 125
Apocrypha, apocryphal, 6, 7, 9, 59, 64, 65, 67, 71, 83, 84, 86, 98, 103, 114
Athanasius, 24
Augustine of Hippo, 24
Aulen, Gustaf, 14

Babylonian exile, 9, 12, 13, 42, 58, 80, 91
Barclay, William, 66
Baruch, 87
Beza, Theodore, 63
Bible, ix, xi, xii, 1, 11, 25, 26, 27–29
  authority of, 19, 20, 21, 22, 35, 38, 40, 42, 46
  composition of, 5–11
  core teachings of, 31–33
  definition of, 3
  and faith formation, 30–31
  as historical product, 4, 27–28, 36, 38, 46
  as inerrant, 35, 38, 40
  influence of, x, 3
  inspiration of, 35, 37–44
  interpretation of, 39, 40, 44–48
  as literature, 1, 39, 46, 47, 54–56
  as metaphor, 28–29
  misuse of, 1–2, 4
  as narrative drama, 15–17
  nature of, 1–5
  reading the, ix, x–xiv, 2, 29–30
  as sacrament, 29
  as sacred, x, 3, 4, 5, 22, 28, 35, 39
  and tradition, 3–5
  versions and translations of, 58–69
  as Word of God, ix, 3, 17, 35
  See also story theology
Bishops' Bible, 64

Calvin, John, 45, 63
canon(ical), 4, 5, 17, 19
  process, 22–24, 39
canon within the canon, 24–25, 47–48
Christian(s), xii, 21, 25, 26, 27, 39
  life, 14–15, 25, 26
Christianity, x, 15, 22, 25, 26
Chronicles, books of, xi, 6, 9, 41, 77–78
Colossians, book of, 10, 109, 111–12
Columbus, Christopher, x
Community Rule, The, 103–4
compassion, 14, 15, 32, 41, 90, 93
conversion, religious, 38, 57–58
Corinthians, books of, 10, 21, 30, 33, 84, 105, 107–8, 116
Countryman, William, 38
Coverdale, Miles, 63

Daniel, book of, 7, 9, 11, 59, 79, 86, 89–90, 97, 124
Dead Sea Scrolls, 60, 103
deuterocanonical. *See* Apocrypha

Index

Deuteronomy, book of, 8, 19, 20, 21, 31, 32, 42, 73–74, 75, 97
Didache, 23
disciple(ship), 15, 100
Dodd, C. H., 66, 68
dualism, 33, 103, 104

Ecclesiastes, book of, 7, 9, 31, 41, 81, 82
English Standard Version, 66
Enlightenment, 26, 46, 55
Ephesians, book of, 10, 51, 84, 109–10, 111
Erasmus, Desiderius, 62, 69
Essenes, 103, 104
Esther, book of, 7, 9, 79, 103
Exodus, book of, xi, 6, 7, 8, 19, 31, 41, 72, 73, 74, 97
exodus, the, 12, 13, 14, 73
Ezekiel, book of, 6, 7, 42, 88–89, 124
Ezra, book of, 7, 9, 59, 78–79, 93

faith and belief, 25
faith and love, 32, 33
faith and works, 32, 118–19
first half of life, 37, 39
fundamentalism, 47

Galatians, book of, 10, 16, 21, 32, 33, 95, 105, 108–9, 116
General (Catholic) Epistles, 117–23
Genesis, book of, 2, 7, 16, 27, 42, 71–72
Geneva Bible, 63, 64
gnostic, gnosticism, 22, 103, 104
God, 37, 39, 56
  faithfulness of, 11, 16
  image of, 27, 31
  kingdom of, 9
  as love, 31, 33
  loving, 31, 69
  panentheistic view of, 48
  as personal, 39–40
Golden Rule, 24
Good News for Modern Man, 67
gospels, 9, 10, 11, 12, 16, 20, 22, 23, 28, 36, 42, 61, 98–99, 104
Great Bible, the, 63, 64
Great Commandment, 24, 31–32
Gutenberg, Johannes, xi

Habakkuk, book of, 6, 7, 94–95
Haggai, book of, 6, 7, 87, 95–96
Hebrew Bible. *See* Old Testament
Hebrews, book of, 10, 11, 22, 23, 31, 73, 117–18
Hendricks, Howard, 51
Herder, Johann G. von, 46
Hillel (rabbi), 24
Holy Spirit, 14, 15, 29, 37, 40, 46, 47, 48, 82, 91, 101, 104, 130
Hosea, book of, 6, 7, 32, 75, 86, 90

incarnation, 25, 56, 57, 58
International Children's Bible, 67
inspiration. *See* Bible, inspiration of
Irwin, James, x
Isaiah, book of, 6, 7, 41, 42, 86–87, 89, 93, 124

James, book of, 10, 11, 23, 31, 32, 42, 109, 117, 118–19
Jefferson Bible, xiii
Jeremiah, book of, 6, 7, 43, 60, 75, 86, 87–88
Jerome, 60
Jesus Christ, 16, 28, 31, 42, 43, 117, 122
  death and resurrection of, 14, 16, 102, 117
  deity of, xiii
  historical, 24
  humanity of, 117, 122, 123
  as Messiah, 10
  return of. *See* Parousia
  and scripture, 20
  as Son of Man, 16, 90
  as Word of God, 101
Job, book of, 7, 9, 31, 79–80, 81
Joel, book of, 6, 7, 91, 92
John, gospel of, xi, 9, 10, 11, 28, 56, 93, 96, 98, 99, 101–2, 104
John, letters of, 10, 11, 22, 23, 32, 33, 117, 122–23
John the Baptist, 97, 99, 103, 104
Jonah, book of, 6, 7, 92–93
Joshua, book of, 6, 7, 8, 31, 74, 75
Jude, book of, 10, 11, 22, 117, 120–22
Judges, 6, 7, 8, 41, 74, 75

136

Index

King James Version, 63, 64, 69
King, Jr., Martin Luther, 91
Kings, books of, 6, 7, 8, 31, 41, 75, 76–77
Knox, John, 56

Lamentations, book of, 7, 9, 86, 88
Leviticus, book of, xi, 6, 7, 8, 19, 20, 32, 72–73, 74
liberalism, 47
Lindbergh, Charles, x
literature, 1, 54, 55
Luke, gospel of, 9, 10, 19, 21, 22, 31, 32, 33, 41, 42, 43, 97, 98, 99, 101–2
Luther, Martin, 45, 62

Maccabees, books of, 7, 9, 65, 90n1
Malachi, book of, 6, 7, 97
Marcion, 23
Mark, gospel of, 9, 21, 31, 43, 97, 98, 99–100, 122
Mary Magdalene, 22
Mary Tudor, 63
Matthew, gospel of, 6, 9, 20, 31, 32, 33, 41, 42, 43, 48, 57, 93, 96, 97, 98, 99, 100, 101, 122
McLaren, Brian, 30
Metzger, Bruce, xi, 121
Micah, book of, 6, 7, 86, 93, 94
Mosaic law. *See* Torah

Nahum, book of, 6, 7, 94
Nehemiah, book of, 7, 9, 59, 78–79, 93, 97
New Century Version, 67
New English Bible, 66
New King James Bible, 65
New Life Version, 68
New Revised Standard Version, 65, 68
New Testament, xii, xiii, 3, 4, 6, 9–11, 15, 16, 17, 23, 42, 43, 49, 58, 102
Numbers, book of, xi, 6, 7, 19, 73–74

Obadiah, book of, 6, 7, 92
Old Testament, xii, xiii, 3, 4, 5–9, 15, 16, 17, 23, 42, 43, 58

Parousia, the, 11, 16, 20, 112–13, 121

Paul (apostle), 4, 10, 11, 19, 21, 24, 30, 32, 42, 43, 95, 101, 104, 105, 117, 119, 120
  letters of, 10, 23, 50, 98, 105-17, 121
Peter, books of, 10, 11, 22, 23, 31, 37, 42, 52, 117, 119–22
Peterson, Eugene H., 69
Philemon, book of, 10, 11, 105, 111, 116–17
Philippians, book of, 10, 31, 105, 110–11
Phillips, J. B., 66
pietism, 47
Postcritical Paradigm, 26–29
Precritical Paradigm, 25, 26, 27
priest, priestly, 12, 13, 14, 15
prophet(s), 8
Proverbs, book of, 7, 9, 31, 32, 41, 81–82, 83, 84
Psalms, book of, 7, 9, 19, 31, 61, 80–81

Reader's Digest Bible, The, xii
Reformation, Protestant, xi, 45, 48, 54, 62
Renaissance, 46, 54
Revelation, book of, xi, xii, 10, 11, 12, 22, 23, 89, 97, 114, 122, 123–25
Revised Standard Version, xii, 65, 66, 67
Rolle, Richard, 61
Romans, book of, 10, 11, 16, 33, 43, 95, 105, 106, 108
Ruth, book of, 7, 9, 75

Samuel, books of, 6, 7, 8, 31, 75, 76, 77
scripture. *See* Bible
second half of life, 39
Sermon on the Mount, 20, 32, 100, 118
Septuagint, 6, 21, 59–60, 83, 103
Sirach (Ecclesiasticus), book of, 7, 71, 81, 83, 103
Song of Songs, book of, 7, 9, 41, 71, 84
story theology, 11–15

Targums, 59, 61, 68
Taylor, Kenneth N., 69
Ten Commandments, 36, 61
The Jerusalem Bible, 68

Index

The Living Bible Paraphrased, 69
The Message, 69
The New American Bible, 68
Thessalonians, books of, 10, 105, 107, 109, 112–13
Thomas, Gospel of, 22, 102–3
Timothy, books of, 10, 31, 37, 52, 105, 114–15, 116
Titus, book of, 10, 31, 105, 114, 115, 116
Tobit, book of, 7, 9, 71, 84–85
Torah, 5, 6, 8, 16, 19, 20, 24–25, 59, 71, 97, 100, 104, 109, 118
translation principle, 56–58

Tyndale, William, 62–63

Vulgate, 60, 61, 62, 64

Walls, Andrew, 56, 57
Wesley, John, 56
Wisdom of Solomon, book of, 7, 23, 42, 71, 81, 82–83
Wycliffe, John, 62

Zechariah, book of, 6, 7, 41, 87, 96–97, 124
Zephaniah, book of, 6, 7, 95

www.ingramcontent.com/pod-product-compliance
Lightning Source LLC
Chambersburg PA
CBHW070913160426
43193CB00011B/1442